THE SYSTEM OF THEOLOGY

CONTAINED IN THE

WESTMINSTER SHORTER CATECHISM.

OPENED AND EXPLAINED.

PART I.—BELIEF CONCERNING GOD.

BY

REV. A. A. HODGE, D. D.

PART II.—DUTY REQUIRED OF MAN.

BY

REV. J. ASPINWALL HODGE, D. D.

PUBLISHERS
Eugene, Oregon

Wipf and Stock Publishers
199 W 8th Ave, Suite 3
Eugene, OR 97401

The System of Theology contained in the Westminster Shorter Catechism
Opened and Explained
By Hodge, A.A. and Hodge, J. Aspinwall
ISBN: 1-59244-809-7
Publication date 8/26/2004
Previously published by A.C. Armstrong and Son, 1888

PREFACE.

There is an increasing desire to know what are the doctrines of Christianity as revealed in the word of God. Laymen, as well as ministers, are recognizing the necessity of having clear views of God's plan of salvation, and of being able to impart them to others.

To quicken and satisfy this desire seems to have been a cherished purpose of Rev. A. A. Hodge, D. D., both as pastor and professor. In the home, church, classroom, by the press and on the platform, he sought to popularize theology. His success was manifest in the numbers who sought to hear him, and in their increasing interest in his instructions. He therefore readily assented when asked to prepare a concise text-book for theological instruction. He naturally determined to make a brief exposition of the Shorter Catechism, for it was prepared by the learned divines of the Westminster Assembly, it is the most comprehensive and accurate statement of Christian doctrine, it is a part of the constitution of our Presbyterian Church, and it is adapted to popular instruction, having been prepared for the young that they might be early taught the truth at home and in the church. Dr. Hodge's sudden death left the work incomplete. He had, however, written Part I., the most important, which sets forth " what man is to believe concerning God." His cousin, J. Aspinwall Hodge, has endeavored to carry out his plan in preparing Part II., which teaches "what duty God requires of man." The whole is now published for general use in the Church, to enable parents to make home instruction intelligent and correct, to encourage the formation of adult classes in the Sabbath-schools for the study of the doctrines of the Church, to furnish our elders with a clear and brief exposition of the system of doctrine which they are required sincerely to receive and adopt, and to give our candidates for the ministry, at the very beginning of their course, a general view, with clear outlines, of God's nature and his gracious plan of salvation, and of man's condition and duty, which they are to devote their lives to study and to preach.

It is earnestly hoped that these ends may be accomplished, and that many will be led "to glorify God and to enjoy him for ever."

J. A. H.

HARTFORD, CONN.

THE SYSTEM OF THEOLOGY

CONTAINED IN

THE WESTMINSTER SHORTER CATECHISM

EXHIBITED AND EXPLAINED.

PART I.

FROM the fourth century the instruction of children and of candidates for baptism comprehended the memorizing and the explanation of the Apostles' Creed, the Ten Commandments, and the Lord's Prayer, together constituting the rule of our faith, of our duties, and of our worship. These became ever after the main materials of elementary religious instruction and the basis of the numerous catechisms which sprang up after the Reformation.

LUTHER's Small Catechism embraces five parts: I. The Ten Commandments. II. The Creed. III. The Lord's Prayer. IV. The Sacrament of Holy Baptism. V. The Sacrament of the Altar.

CALVIN's Catechism (Geneva, 1541) was divided into five parts as follows: I. Of Faith, an exposition of the Creed. II. Of the Law, the Ten Commandments. III. Of Prayer. IV. Of the Word of God. V. Of the Sacraments.

The ANGLICAN (Episcopal) Catechism observes the

6   THE WESTMINSTER SYSTEM OF DOCTRINE.

following order: The Creed; The Ten Commandments; The Lord's Prayer; Baptism; The Lord's Supper.

The ROMAN Catechism, prepared by the order of the Council of Trent, follows the order of—1, The Creed; 2, The Sacraments; 3, The Ten Commandments; 4, The Lord's Prayer.

The HEIDELBERG Catechism observes the following order: *First Part.* Man's Misery. *Second Part.* Man's Redemption, and under this the Creed and the Sacraments. *Third Part.* Of Thankfulness, including the Ten Commandments and the Lord's Prayer.

Our own Catechism, prepared by the learned divines of the Westminster Assembly, is a much more accurate and comprehensive statement of Christian truth than any of these. Dr. Schaff says that "it is one of the three typical Catechisms of Protestantism which are likely to last to the end of time. It is fully equal to Luther's and to the Heidelberg Catechism in ability and influence, it far surpasses them in clearness and careful wording, and is better adapted to the Scotch and Anglo-American mind, but it lacks their genial warmth, freshness, and childlike simplicity." Richard Baxter called it "the best Catechism I ever saw, a most excellent sum of the Christian faith and doctrine, and a fit test to try the orthodoxy of teachers." It like the others is also founded on the traditional group of lessons, the Creed, the Ten Commandments, and the Lord's Prayer, common to all Church Catechisms. It observes the following order:

I. INTRODUCTION. Questions 1–3.

II. WHAT ARE WE TO BELIEVE? Questions 4–38.

III. WHAT DUTY IS REQUIRED OF US? Questions 39–81.

THE INTRODUCTION. 7

IV. THE LAW FAILS BECAUSE OF SIN, all men are guilty and helpless. Questions 82–84.

V. MEANS AND CONDITIONS OF SALVATION. Questions 85–107.

Internal Means. Faith and Repentance. Questions 85–87.

Outward Means. The Word, the Sacraments and Prayer. Questions 88–107.

I. THE INTRODUCTION. Questions 1–3.

Q. 1. *What is the chief end of man?*

A. *Man's chief end is to glorify God, and to enjoy him for ever.*

Q. 2. *What rule hath God given to direct us how we may glorify and enjoy him?*

A. *The* WORD OF GOD, *which is contained in the Scriptures, of the Old and New Testaments, is the only rule to direct us how we may glorify and enjoy him.*

Q. 3. *What do the Scriptures principally teach?*

A. *The Scriptures principally teach what man is to believe concerning God, and what duty God requires of man.*

The Shorter Catechism presupposes natural religion. The light of nature and the "law written on man's heart" teach us that there is a God, and that he is a powerful, wise, and righteous person. The "chief end" of man is God's ultimate design in his creation, which is manifested and proved by man's moral and rational constitution, and the intuitions with which he is endowed by his Creator.

All religion, revealed as well as natural, rests ultimately upon man's moral and religious constitution. Our intuitions of right and wrong, of spiritual beauty, etc., are just as certain as our sense perceptions. Revealed religion adds to the religion of nature the testimonies of God's Word and Spirit. But if man's reason and moral sense are not reliable, the Scriptures have no organ to appeal to, and no test by which to prove their own divine origin. The Shorter Catechism therefore—

1st. IN QUESTION FIRST affirms that by nature man is a religious being, created with the ultimate design of promoting the glory of God, and so constituted as to find his highest and permanent blessedness in his communion and service. The *first* of the great corner-stones upon which the theology of our Catechism rests is, consequently, the religious nature and endowments of man and the validity of his moral and spiritual intuitions. Revealed Religion takes for granted natural religion, guarantees and supplements its truths. The design or purpose of the Maker in his work is always the chief end of the work, and in every case this purpose must be known in order to understand the nature of the work. The first question in every case must be, What is the thing for ? Our understanding of the entire system of revealed truth, therefore, depends upon the view taken of the ultimate end or design of God in creating, preserving, and redeeming mankind. The Scriptures and our Confession of Faith agree in teaching that the manifestation of his own glory is the great chief end of God in all he has done—(1) of his purposes: (Eph. 1 : 5, 6, 12 ; Conf. of Faith, ch. 3, §§ 3, 5); (2) of his works of Creation (Col. 1 : 16 ; Rom. 11 : 36 ; Rev. 4 : 11 ; Conf. Faith, ch. 4, § 1); (3) of his works of Providence and Redemption (Rom. 9 : 17, 22, 23 ; Eph. 3 : 10 ; Conf.

Faith, ch. 5, § 1); (4) and the chief aim of the creatures in all holy service (1 Cor. 10 : 31 ; 1 Pet. 4 : 11).

2d. IN QUESTION SECOND the Catechism lays down the second great corner-stone of our faith and the principal source of our religious knowledge—the fact that God has spoken to man directly, and that his Word is contained in the Scriptures of the Old and New Testament, and that in his present condition this WORD OF GOD alone is an infallible rule of what we are to believe and what we are to do.

[I.] The Scriptures of the Old and New Testaments are the two collections of inspired writings which God commissioned prophets and apostles to write and give to his Church respectively under the Old or Mosaic and under the New or Christian Dispensations, or modes of administering the Covenant of Grace. A list of the several books contained in these two testaments is given in the first chapter of our Confession of Faith.

The *canon* of Scripture is that sacred *rule* of faith and practice which is composed of all the genuine writings of the inspired prophets and apostles now extant. The fact that all the books now contained in our canon of the Old Testament are genuine, and they only, is proved. 1. Christ and his apostles approve as genuine and authentic the Jewish Hebrew canon as it existed in their time. They often quote these books, and only these, and rebuke the Jews for disobeying them (Mark 14 : 49; Luke 24 : 44; John 5 : 39; 2 Tim. 3 : 15, 16; Acts 1 : 16; Matt. 22 : 29). 2. The Hebrew canon thus endorsed by Christ is the same that we now have. This is proved by the Hebrew text kept with such jealous care by the Jews, by the Septuagint version made in Egypt, B. C. 285, and by the testimony of Josephus and of the early Christian writers. The fact that the several writings composing our New-Testament canon are genuine and authentic is proved—1. By the testimony of early Christian writers, from the age of the apostles downward. 2. By the list of books received of them as canonical made by the early Church Fathers. 3. By the early translations, such as the Peshito, or early Syriac version (about end of second century), and the Vulgate, prepared by Jerome, A. D. 385, based upon the early Latin version. 4. By the internal evidence of language, idiom, style of the several books, and their consistency, with their historic conditions and with the doctrinal spirit and unity of the whole.

[II.] This canon of Scripture as we possess it IS THE WORD OF GOD. This is expressly affirmed (Conf. Faith, ch. 1, § 2; L. Cat., Q. 3; Form of Government, ch. 15, § 12, 1). It is so called because the whole of it, matter and form, is the product of men who were commissioned to speak to us in God's name and by his authority (Matt. 10 : 19, 20; 28 : 19, 20; Luke 10 : 16; 12 : 12; John 13 : 20; 14 : 26; 15 : 26, 27), and were qualified for this tremendous responsibility by the continued influence of the Holy Spirit. REVELATION is the work of the Holy Ghost communicating to men, by supernatural means, new truth. This is a large element of the sacred Scriptures. INSPIRATION is the continuous influence of the Holy Ghost upon the sacred writers in the act of writing the Word of God to men, so that they were directed to write the very truth God designed, and prevented from all error in doing so. This inspiration extends equally to all portions of Scripture, so that all come to us with the divine authority, and constitute an

THE APOSTLES, CREED. 11

absolutely errorless rule of faith and practice (Heb. 3 : 7; Acts 2 : 17; 4 : 25; Heb. 1 : 1; 2 Tim. 3 : 16; Matt. 5 : 18; Luke 24 : 44; 1 Thess. 2 : 13; 2 Cor. 13 : 2–4; Gal. 1 : 8, 9). And this inspiration extends to the words of Scripture—*i. e.* to the original words, whenever by diligent examination of ancient copies these can be ascertained and the errors of transcription corrected (1 Cor. 2 : 13; compare Gal. 3 : 16 and Gen. 17 : 7). " The authority of the Holy Scripture, for which it ought to be believed and obeyed, dependeth not upon the testimony of any man or Church, but wholly upon God (who is truth itself), the Author thereof; and therefore it is to be received, BECAUSE IT IS THE WORD OF GOD" (Confession of Faith, ch. 1, § 4).

THESE INSPIRED SCRIPTURES incidentally contain much history and prophecy, and hence throw light both upon the past and future of mankind. But their principal design is to teach us—(1) What we are to believe as to God and his relations and purposes as to us; and (2) What duties God requires of us. Ques. 3d.

II. WHAT DO THE SCRIPTURES REQUIRE US TO BELIEVE CONCERNING GOD, AND HIS RELATIONS TO US, AND HIS PURPOSES WITH REGARD TO US? Ques. 4–38.

All the ancient Catechisms, as well as that of Luther and the Heidelberg Catechism, answer this general question by presenting and expounding the Apostles' Creed, which is adopted by all the Roman, Lutheran, and Calvinistic churches. This Creed is not made part of this Catechism, but is appended to it, together with the Lord's

Prayer and Ten Commandments, and is part of the authoritative Confession of the Presbyterian Church.

This venerable Creed presents the objects of the Christian's faith and the ground of his hope rather as historical facts, in an historical order, than as a system of abstract doctrines. Thus:

I believe in God the Father almighty, maker of heaven and earth; and in Jesus Christ, his only Son, our Lord; who was conceived by the Holy Ghost, born of the Virgin Mary; suffered under Pontius Pilate, was crucified, dead, and buried, he descended unto hell:* the third day he rose again from the dead; he ascended unto heaven, and sitteth on the right hand of God the Father Almighty; from thence he shall come to judge the quick and the dead. I believe in the Holy Ghost; the holy catholic Church; the communion of saints; the forgiveness of sins; the resurrection of the body; and the life everlasting. Amen.

THE SHORTER CATECHISM, on the other hand, sets forth the matter of Christian faith in a series of propositions arranged in a logical order.

All theology is concerned with the self-revelation of God which he has made in his Word, and it embraces three great divisions: (1) God's existence and nature; (2) God's will or plan; and (3) God's works in execution of his plan.

---

* ῟Αιδης was the common term for the invisible spirit-world, to which the good and the wicked both went, the former to a state of holy happiness in Abraham's bosom, the other to torment. The human spirit of Christ went, while his body was in the grave, precisely where all the spirits of Old-Testament saints were waiting for him. By going there he changed it into heaven. Heaven is where Christ is. To be in heaven is to be "*present with the Lord*" (2 Cor. 5:8).

[I.] God's Existence. Ques. 4–6.

1st. AS TO HIS NATURE AND ATTRIBUTES.

Q. 4. *What is God?*

A. *God is a Spirit, infinite, eternal, and unchangeable, in his being, wisdom, power, holiness, justice, goodness, and truth.*

This is the best definition of God ever written. It is founded on the revealed fact that he created man in his own image. We hence ascribe to him in absolute perfection and unlimited degree everything that we find an excellence in ourselves, and we deny of him every defect and limitation that we find in ourselves. He can have no bodily parts or passions, for they would limit his greatness and his power. He is therefore a SPIRIT— that is, a holy intelligent person possessing all the essential perfections of the human spirit. Wisdom, holiness, goodness, truth in him are precisely what they are in us, except as they are made more excellent by the great distinguishing predicates of infinitude, eternity, and immutability, for these qualify all his being and all his properties. He is infinite, eternal, unchangeable in his being or substance, and also in his wisdom, and also in his power, and also in his holiness, etc., etc.

The indefinite is that to which we place no bounds. The infinite is that to which no limits can be placed. God is infinite.

He is infinite as to duration. Time is limited duration, measured by successions either of thought or motion. God exists beyond all limits of time, without beginning, without end, without succession. There is no past or future; all duration is always present to Him.

He is infinite as to space. He is not extended nor divided nor multiplied, but the whole God is present everywhere at every moment.

God's wisdom is absolutely perfect because his knowledge is infinite. Wisdom includes knowledge, and implies the perfectly right use of unlimited knowledge. He knows himself, and all things outside of himself, by one eternal absolutely perfect act of intuition. He does not reason from the known to the unknown, but he beholds all existence past, present, and future by one act as a whole. He knows all things in their essences as they really are, not merely as they appear, and he knows them in all their properties and relations and with infallible accuracy.

God's power is infinite because by his pure will he can do anything he chooses either with or without or against second causes as he pleases. He is in his works of creation and providence entirely free from all hindrance or limitation from anything outside himself. He cannot act inconsistently with his own perfections. This is his only limit.

God's holiness is absolutely perfect. There is no conflict, no limit, no deficiency, no exaggeration in his moral perfection. The love of righteousness and the hatred of iniquity are his most characteristic and controlling principles. They are the foundation of his being and of all his plans and works. The justice of God is absolute and immutable, and without limit. He is just in making and in executing laws as King of the moral world. He is just in all his relations and dealings with his moral subjects. He is immutably determined by the moral perfection of his nature to visit every sin with a just recompense of reward, if not in the person of the sinner, then in the person of his Substitute. The terrible lake of fire and the cross of Calvary are awful testimonies to his absolute justice.

The goodness of God is absolute and measureless. Toward all sentient creatures it is exercised as benevolence and beneficence. Toward all holy persons it is exercised as love. Toward all suffering creatures it goes out as mercy. Toward sinners of the human family it is exercised as grace. It is obvious that absolute justice demands satisfaction independently of the personal discretion of the Judge, but grace from its essential nature must be sovereign, and depends absolutely upon the free will of the King.

The truth of God is absolutely perfect, and has no limits. It is the foundation of all knowledge, all action, and all faith. God is self-consistent—*i. e.* true to himself. He is unchangeable—*i. e.* true to his past, and to all his plans, and to all his pledges. He is infallibly correct in all his revelations and reliable in all his engagements. Therefore we trust the testimony of our senses and the deductions of our reason, for he made us. Therefore we believe the Bible because it is his WORD.

2d. GOD IS ONE GOD, YET THREE PERSONS. Ques. 5 and 6.

Q. 5. *Are there more Gods than one?*

A. *There is but one only, the living and true God.*

Q. 6. *How many persons are there in the Godhead?*

A. *There are three persons in the Godhead; the Father, the Son, and the Holy Ghost; and these three are one God, the same in substance, equal in power and glory.*

The doctrine of the Personality of God is taught in the Bible under the following heads:

A. *There is but one God.*—The unity of the world shows there is only one Maker. The voice of conscience testifies that there is only one Lord and Master. Reason teaches that there can be but one infinite and absolute Sovereign. This one God is called the living and true God, to distinguish his name from those of the false gods the heathen worship, who are false and dead. Hence God is one spirit—*i. e.* one substance—and Father, Son, and Holy Ghost, being that one and selfsame substance, have the same attributes, and are of course equal in power and glory.

B. *Father, Son, and Holy Ghost are all this one living and true God.*

None can doubt that this is true as to the Father. The Bible abundantly proves that (1) the Son is truly God; (2) the Holy Spirit is a distinct person.

1st. *The Son is Truly God.*—The proof of the divinity of Christ virtually establishes the doctrine of the Trinity: (1) He existed before his birth from the Virgin (John 8 : 58; 17 : 5; 3 : 31). (2) All the names and titles of God are habitually given to him (John 1 : 1; 1 John 5 : 20; Rom. 9 : 5; Rev. 1 : 8). (3) All divine attributes are predicated of him: *eternity* (John 8 : 58); *immutability* (Heb. 1 : 10, 11; 13 : 8); *omnipresence* (Matt. 18 : 20; John 3 : 13); *omniscience* (Matt. 11 : 27); *omnipotence* (John 5 : 17; Heb. 1 : 3). (4) All divine works are asserted of him: *Creation* (John 1 : 3–10); *preservation and providential government* (Col. 1 : 17); *judgment* (John 5 : 22; Matt. 25 : 31, 32); *giving eternal life* (John 10 :

28); sending the Holy Ghost (John 16 : 7). (5) Divine worship is to be paid to him (Heb. 1 : 6 ; Rev. 1 : 5, 6).

2d. *The Holy Ghost is a Distinct Person.*—Christ uses all the personal pronouns, I, thou, he, when speaking of the relation of the Spirit to himself and to the Father (John 14: 17, 26; 15 : 26). The Spirit acts as a Person, "teaching," "interceding," "dividing to every man as he wills" (John 16 : 7–14 ; Rom. 8 : 26 ; 1 Cor. 12 : 11). We are "baptized into his name" as "into the name of the Father." He may be grieved, and wicked men commit "blasphemy against the Holy Ghost" (Eph. 4 : 30 ; Matt. 12 : 31, 32).

C. Father, Son, and Holy Ghost are distinct Persons. They love one another. They speak to and of one another. They send and are sent by one another. They take counsel together and work together to one common end (John 14 : 16, 26 ; 15 : 26 ; 16 : 13–15 ; 17 : 5, 6).

D. They are eternally and mutually related as Father, and Son, and Spirit. The Father is first, the Son second, and the Spirit third. The First is Father of the Second. The Second is "Son," is the "Word," the "Express Image," the "Fullness bodily," of the First. The Third is the Spirit of the Father and of the Son.

E. In all their outward work on the creation they work together according to one plan. The Father sends the Son and the Spirit. The Father and Son send the Spirit. The Son reveals the Father. The Spirit everywhere operates and executes the common will of Father, Son, and Holy Ghost.

F. In the work of redemption the Scriptures attribute the *sovereign plan* to the Father, the *execution* to the Son, the *application* to the Holy Spirit. *"Through* him

(Christ) we have access (introduction) *by* one Spirit *unto* the Father" (Eph. 2 : 18).

THE NICENE CREED, COMPOSED 325 A. D.

I believe in one God, the Father Almighty, Maker of heaven and earth, and of all things visible and invisible:

And in one Lord Jesus Christ, the only-begotten Son of God, begotten of his Father before all worlds, God of God, Light of Light, Very God of Very God, begotten, not made, Being of one substance with the Father; by whom all things were made; who for us men, and for our salvation, came down from heaven, and was incarnate by the Holy Ghost of the Virgin Mary, and was made man, and was crucified for us under Pontius Pilate. He suffered and was buried, and the third day he rose again according to the Scriptures, and ascended into heaven, and sitteth on the right hand of the Father. And he shall come again with glory to judge both the quick and the dead; whose kingdom shall have no end.

And I believe in the Holy Ghost, the Lord and Giver of life, who proceedeth from the Father and the Son, who with the Father and the Son together is worshipped and glorified, who spake by the prophets. And I believe in one Catholic and Apostolic Church. I acknowledge one baptism for the remission of sins, and I look for the resurrection of the dead and the life of the world to come.

[II.] God's Will or Plan. Ques. 7.

Q. 7. *What are the Decrees of God?*

A. *The Decrees of God are, his eternal purpose according to the counsel of his will, whereby, for his own glory, he hath foreordained whatsoever comes to pass.*

The Scriptures refer the Plan of God pre-eminently to the Father, but essentially to the whole Godhead (John 10 : 18; 12 : 49; 17 : 6). If God is an intelligent agent, he must have had a plan; if an eternal, infinitely wise and powerful and immutable agent, he must have had one all-comprehensive plan from the beginning; if he exists as three Persons, his plan must be mutual—that is, of the nature of a covenant, to be executed by the Three in concert.

The Plan must have the attributes of the Planner. It must be absolutely righteous, benevolent, and just. It must be absolutely sovereign and immutable. The purposes of the Planner are not the proximate causes of any thing; nevertheless, they must infallibly be fulfilled.

They are *one* purpose. We speak of "decrees" because, being finite, we necessarily think only of one small part of his plan at a time. But to his mind and will it is only one single plan, embracing as one system all the ends, means, and conditions of events in their natural relations. It establishes the dependence of ends on means and conditions, so that these can never be separated. The liberty of free agents and the contingency of second causes are included in God's decree, and therefore can never be interfered with by it. (Compare the 24th and 31st vs. of 27th chap. of Acts.) This one all-comprehensive decree is necessary if God infallibly *foreknows* whatsoever will come to pass. For if he foresees how any man will act in a given conjuncture, and so foreseeing proceeds to create him and place him in that conjuncture, he, of course, in so doing predetermines the occurrence of the event. But the event itself is no less free, being produced solely by the rational, unbound will of the man himself.

This Plan must be sovereign, since God alone exists when he forms it, and all things that afterward exist are made what they are by the Plan itself. And for the same reason the single great end of the Plan is the glory of God himself; that is, the manifestation of his inherent excellence by the exercise of his perfections. If the glory of God is the chief end of the Plan, it must, of course, be the chief end of every part of it—of creation, of providence, and of redemption; and so the Scriptures declare.

This Plan, being universal, must include the designed and deliberate permission of sin, and the determination to overrule it to the end of his own glory. But God cannot be the cause of sin. The only cause of sin is the rebellious wills of his creatures. The Scriptures assign to God only these relations to sin: (1) he abhors it; (2) he forbids it; (3) he permits it; (4) he restrains it; (5) he punishes it; (6) he overrules its consequences to good (Ps. 76 : 10 ; Acts 2 : 23 ; 4 : 27, 28).

(See Dan. 4 : 35 ; Isa. 40 : 13, 14 ; Rom. 9 : 15, 18 ; Eph. 1 : 5, 11 ; Matt. 11 : 25, 26.)

Since the salvation of guilty sinners is absolutely of free and sovereign GRACE, and must be received as such, the salvation of every man must depend upon a personal election of God. God *offers* salvation to all on the condition of faith. But he gives the faith to those whom he chooses (Eph. 2 : 8 ; Matt. 20 : 16 ; 22 : 14). Nevertheless, those who refuse to believe and be saved have only themselves to blame for it, because the only reason they do not believe is the wicked disposition of their

GOD'S WORKS OF CREATION. 21

own hearts, and because God kindly and honestly invites them and promises salvation by his Word, and draws them by the common influences of his Spirit.

But those whom God punishes he punishes not as Sovereign, but as Judge, justly for their sin. He "ordains them to dishonor and wrath for their sin, to the praise of his glorious justice" (Conf. Faith, chap. 3, § 7; Larger Cat., Q. 13; Lam. 3 : 22; John 3 : 16; Rom. 3 : 24; 11 : 5, 6; 1 Cor. 4 : 7; 15 : 10; Eph. 1 : 5, 6; 2 : 4-10).

[III.] The Execution of God's Plan. Ques. 8–38.

Q. 8. *How doth God execute his Decrees?*

A. *God executeth his Decrees in the works* (1) *of Creation and* (2) *Providence.*

A. GOD'S WORKS OF CREATION. Ques. 9, 10.
FIRST. GENERAL CREATION.

Q. 9. *What is the work of creation?*

A. *The work of creation is God's making all things of nothing, by the word of his power, in the space of six days, and all very good.*

In the beginning of time God first, by a word of command, brought into being all the material elements of which the universe exists. Then all was chaos, an abyss without form and void, and dark. Then the divine Spirit brought gradually, through a process called genesis, during successive periods of duration, cycles, or ages, the elements into order, and so produced the suns and planets and all things therein in their generations. The "days" of creation are supposed to have been long periods of time, the measure of which is not known to us. There was a time when the world was not, and God existed alone (Gen. ch. 1–ch. 2 : 3; Ps. 90 : 2; John 17 : 5, 24; Heb. 11 : 3; Ps. 33 : 6; 148 : 5).

A distinction must be made between God's *immediate* creation of the material elements out of nothing, and his *mediate* creation of new species of things out of materials already existing. Thus, God formed the bodies of men and of beasts *out of the ground*, and the soul of man he produced by breathing into him life (Gen. 2 : 7 and 19). We believe that God creates all immaterial souls immediately and severally out of nothing.

The fact that God is said to have rested from his labors on the seventh day (Gen. 2 : 2, 3) does not by any means prove that he made all things in the universe at one time or in one series, or that he has not often, and may not now and hereafter, exercise his power both of immediate and mediate creation. (See John 5 : 17.)

All things were good, because each after its kind and in its relations was perfectly adapted to the end for which God created it.

SECOND. THE SPECIAL CREATION OF MAN. Ques. 10.

Q. 10. *How did God create man?*

A. *God created man male and female, after his own image, in knowledge, righteousness, and holiness, with dominion over the creatures.*

"After God had made all other creatures, he created man, male and female, with reasonable and immortal souls, endued with knowledge, righteousness, and true holiness, after his own image, having the law of God written in their hearts, and power to fulfill it; and yet under a possibility of transgressing, being left to the liberty of their own will, which was subject unto change" (Conf. Faith, chap. 4, § 2).

Man has existed in *four* states—(1) Adam and Eve, as created by God, were holy, disposed to and able to do right, yet mutable and also able to do wrong. This state was peculiar to Adam and Eve, and experienced by them alone of all mankind.

(2) Their descendants since the fall have corrupt natures, and are, before they are born again by the Holy Ghost, utterly unable to wish, or to begin, or to do anything spiritually good—*i. e.* pertaining to their relations to God. They are free in willing evil, but not able to will that which is good.

(3) In the new birth God frees the Christian from the bondage of corruption, and enables him by divine assistance freely to will that which is right; but by reason of the remains of sin in his imperfect state of sanctification in this life he freely wills at times both evil and good. But through grace the good is made to triumph.

(4) "The will of man is made perfectly and immutably free to good alone in the state of glory only" (Conf. Faith, chap. 9, §§ 2–5).

In opposition to the modern doctrine of evolution that man has worked up from the condition of an animal to moral agency, and from bestiality, through savagery and barbarism, to civilization, the whole Bible doctrine of sin and redemption, running through both Testaments, maintains the following points: (1) Man was created holy, but mutable. (2) He had a fair trial in a pure world and with an easy and reasonable test. (3) He voluntarily sinned and corrupted his nature. (4) Hence he is polluted, guilty, and helpless. (5) Hence the necessity of the expiation of guilt by the blood of Christ, and of the removal of pollution and helplessness by the Holy Ghost.

That God made Adam holy is proved (1) from Scripture (Gen. 1 : 26 ; Col. 3 : 10 ; Eph. 4 : 24 ; Eccles. 7 : 29). (2) From reason. If God did not make Adam holy, he never could have become so. (Moral character comes before moral action. The tree must be made good in order that the fruit should be good. A holy being might produce sin through selfishness, appetite, or inattention. But holiness could never originate in moral indifference, which in a moral being is itself sin. The double phrase in Gen. 1 : 26, "in our image" and "after our likeness," simply intensifies the emphasis.

This likeness to God, which of course applies only to the soul and not to the body of man, is of two kinds:

1. The constitutional likeness as a rational, moral, voluntary spirit. *This* likeness man never has lost, and never can lose in any world.

2. The moral and spiritual likeness, consisting in spiritual knowledge, righteousness, and true holiness, which the children of Adam have all lost in his fall, and which is restored to all believers in Christ by the Holy Ghost in their regeneration and sanctification.

The "dominion" of man over the creatures (Gen. 1 : 26) partly results from man's "constitutional likeness to God," which he has not lost; that is, from his superior intelligence. But for the absolute sanction of this right, and for its unlimited exercise, all must wait until our nature is completely "renewed in knowledge (and true holiness) after the image of Him that created him" (Eph. 4 : 24 and Col. 3 : 10).

B. GOD'S WORKS OF PROVIDENCE.

Q. 11. *What are God's works of Providence?*

A. *God's works of Providence are his most holy, wise, and powerful, preserving and governing all his creatures and all their actions.*

The title PROVIDENCE includes all God's activities in relation to his creatures of every kind subsequent to their creation.

It is exercised in various ways: 1st. His *natural* Providence over all things and elements embraced in the material universe. 2d. His *moral* Providence, or moral government over all his intelligent and moral creatures. 3d. His *supernatural* Providence, embracing his entire work of Redemption, embracing the Incarnation of God in human nature, the Revelation of truth and the Inspiration of the prophets and apostles, and miracles to authenticate their divine commission, and the gracious work of the Holy Ghost in the hearts of his redeemed people. Nevertheless, this PROVIDENCE in its widest comprehension is one harmonious system, whereby the natural, the moral, and the supernatural fit and work together: the moral is built upon the natural, and the supernatural built upon the moral.

This *Providence*, in its general sense, includes—1st, a Plan. This Plan is God's all-comprehensive Decree, discussed under the last section. It is one intellectual system, logically coherent in all its parts, comprehending in one system all beings and events in all worlds, material and spiritual, natural and supernatural.

2d. Providence includes God's preserving all his creatures. This means that as no creature can bring itself into being, so no creature can continue to exist a single moment unless upheld by the almighty power of God. Nothing except God is self-existent. All created existence for ever continues to be dependent existence. "By him all things consist;" "Upholding all things by the word of his power;" "In him we live and move and have our being" (Col. 1 : 17 ; Heb. 1 : 3 ; Acts 17 : 28). 3d. Lastly, this general PROVIDENCE of God consists in his governing all his creatures and all their actions. This government of God is accomplished by him —A. As *immanent* in all things as our souls are in our bodies, whereby at the same time, and equally in all things and places, he acts immediately in every atom of matter and upon the centre of every spirit *from within* outward. B. This divine government is accomplished by God as a *transcendent* Person external to his creatures, commanding, threatening, punishing, inviting, promising, and acting upon the creature on occasion *from without.*

This providential government must—1st. Be consistent with the nature of God—*i. e.* be "holy, wise, and powerful," and abundantly merciful. 2d. It must always be consistent with the nature of each one of the creatures severally affected thereby—*i. e.* he governs material bodies in consistency with the laws of matter; living bodies in consistency with the laws of life; brute animals in consistency with their natural instincts; and men and angels in consistency with their rational natures and with the freedom of their wills. He works *in* the wills of men *from within*, making them "willing in the day of his power," and working in them "to will and to do"—first to will, and then to do—"of his good pleasure." And he also works *on* the wills of men *from without*, by presenting motives, arguments, persuasions

THE COVENANT WITH ADAM. 27

threatenings, promises, appeals to reason and to conscience, etc. Thus he governs while the wills of men remain perfectly free and responsible.

This providential government embraces all things, material and spiritual, temporal and eternal, in one system. "After a most special manner it taketh care of his Church, and disposeth all things to the good thereof," and of every member thereof (Rom. 8 : 28). The final end of his providential government in all its departments is the manifestation of his own glory (Rom. 9 : 17; 11 : 36).

C. GOD'S SPECIAL PROVIDENCE TOWARD MANKIND AT THEIR CREATION.

Q. 12. *What special act of Providence did God exercise toward man in the estate wherein he was created?*

A. *When God had created man, he entered into a covenant of life with him, upon condition of perfect obedience; forbidding him to eat of the tree of knowledge of good and evil, upon pain of death.*

God having made man holy, yet mutable and liable to fall, as shown under Ques. 10, he proceeded mercifully to enter into a Covenant with Adam and Eve as the representatives of the entire mass of their descendants, wherein they were afforded an opportunity of securing, by a temporary obedience during a period of probation under the most favorable circumstances possible, the establishment of their holy character, so that they should never be liable to sin for ever. Thus by one trial would the eternal blessedness of the whole human family have been secured.

A covenant is a conditional promise. God promised to Adam eternal life on condition of his remaining perfectly obedient during a period of probation. The alternative to the promise was death on condition of disobedience. This covenant was called a Covenant of Life, because its promise was life. It has been called, in contrast with the gospel Covenant of Salvation on condition of faith, a Covenant of Works, because its condition was works; and a Legal Covenant, because it demanded as the condition of favor the complete conformity of Adam and all his exercises of soul and body to the law of absolute moral perfection.

The special test of obedience which God selected to try the loyalty of our first parents was expressed in the command not to eat of the fruit of the tree of knowledge of good and evil. This tree, of course, had no moral quality, nor any power of communicating any moral quality in itself. It was called the tree of the knowledge of good and evil because it was used as an instrument to test the fidelity of Adam and Eve, and hence became to them the occasion of that tremendous experience of good and evil which they have subsequently gathered.

God has attached to every one of his covenants with men a visible seal. The use of a seal is to confirm and consummate a contract, and hence to convey to the recipient party the benefits engaged for. The seal of the Covenant God formed with Noah, in which he promised that the earth should never again be destroyed by a flood (Gen. 9 : 9–17), was the rainbow. The seal of the Covenant God made with Abraham, promising that by his seed should all the nations of the earth be blessed (Gen. 12 : 3; 18 : 18; 17 : 1–14), was circumcision. The seal of the Covenant God made with the nation of Israel through Moses was the Passover (Ex. 13 : 3–10). The seals of the gospel Covenant which God makes in Christ

THE FALL OF ADAM. 29

with believers are Baptism and the Lord's Supper. The seal of the Covenant of Works which God made with Adam, and with all mankind in him, was the "TREE OF LIFE" (Gen. 3 : 22, 24).

All these seals are sacraments. The tree of Life had no more inherent power of giving life than the Lord's Supper. But it was requisite to justice and order that Adam and Eve, having broken the covenant, should be excluded from the seal which sacramentally signified, sealed, and conveyed its forfeited benefits.

The Old Testament opens with a view of the Paradise Lost. The New Testament closes with a view of the Paradise Regained, with the "Tree of Life" on either side of the "pure River of Water of Life, clear as crystal, proceeding out of the throne of God and of the Lamb" (Rev. 22 : 1, 2). Thus, "where sin abounded, grace did much more abound" (Rom. 5 : 20).

D. THE FALL OF ADAM AND ITS CONSEQUENCES.
Ques. 13–19.

This includes (1) The origin of sin;

(2) The nature of sin;

(3) The apostatizing act of Adam and Eve;

(4) The way in which their posterity were responsible for that act;

(5) The estate of sin into which that act of apostasy brought all mankind;

(6) The estate of misery which is inseparable from that estate of sin.

1st. THE ORIGIN OF SIN. Ques. 13.

Q. 13. *Did our first parents continue in the estate wherein they were created?*

A. *Our first parents being left to the freedom of their own will, fell from the estate wherein they were created, by sinning against God.*

God is self-existent. All beings other than himself are brought into being by the free act of God creating them. God, being infinitely holy and righteous, cannot be the cause of sin. But, as shown above under Ques. 10, Adam was brought into existence with a nature inclined to holiness, and a will able to choose either obedience or disobedience. He freely chose disobedience, and so sin originated, as it only could originate, in the free act of a free agent. It was at the beginning a voluntary act against sufficient knowledge. It was a free, inexcusable act of rebellion against the All-perfect and the All-beneficent.

2d. THE NATURE OF SIN. Ques. 14.

Q. 14. *What is sin?*

A. *Sin is any want of conformity unto, or transgression, of the law of God.*

The "Law of God" is his holy will, expressing his holy nature however or in whatever form it may be made known to his intelligent and free creatures.

This includes (1) "the law written in their hearts" (Rom. 2:15); (2) the revelation of God in nature (Rom. 1:19, 20); (3) the various personal revelations God made of his will to the prophets in former times (Heb. 1:1); (4) the various revelations God has made of his will in the Scriptures: (*a*) temporary and binding on a single people, as the ceremonial law given for a time to the Jews; (*b*) the universal and permanent moral law, summarily stated in the Ten Commandments; (*c*) all the permanent directions contained in the New Testament

SIN, AND THE FIRST SIN. 31

for the guidance of his people during the present dispensation.

Holiness in the creature is the perfect conformity to this law, as far as made known to him, in his character, his affections, dispositions, purposes, choices, words, and actions. Sin, on the other hand, is any and every want of conformity to this law, as far as made known to him, in his character, his affections, dispositions, purposes, choices, thoughts, words, and actions.

Hence the answer in the Catechism distinguishes between " want of conformity unto " and " transgression of the law of God." This is intended to show—(1) That sin does not exclusively consist of actions, but that the permanent character and inward dispositions and affections of a man when not conformed to the law of God are sinful no less than evil actions. (2) This shows that omissions, failures, and defects in duty are sin as truly as positive transgression.

All sin involves—1st, moral pollution; 2d, guilt, ill-desert, obligation to punishment.

3d. THE APOSTATIZING ACT OF ADAM AND EVE. Ques. 15.

Q. 15. *What was the sin whereby our first parents fell from the estate wherein they were created?*

A. *The sin whereby our first parents fell from the estate wherein they were created, was their eating the forbidden fruit.*

This outward act would have been innocent in itself if it had not been forbidden. God mercifully and justly selected an action in itself morally indifferent, in order that it might be (1) an easy, (2) a thorough and clear test of the simple obedience of Adam and Eve.

The sin was one of disobedience. The incitives to it were (1) the natural attractiveness of the fruit appealing to natural appetite; (2) the seduction of Satan appealing to the weaknesses of the unconfirmed moral nature of our first parents.

The *first* address of the Tempter suggested doubt: " Yea hath God said?" etc. His *second* address suggested positive unbelief: " Ye shall *not* surely die, for," etc. Thus doubt, unbelief, and pride appear to have been the evil states of heart which led to the outward act of disobedience.

4th. THE WAY IN WHICH THEIR POSTERITY WERE RESPONSIBLE FOR THAT ACT. Ques. 16.

Q. 16. *Did all mankind fall in Adam's first transgression?*

A. *The Covenant being made with Adam, not only for himself, but for his posterity, all mankind descending from him by ordinary generation, sinned in him and fell with him in his first transgression.*

The nature of the Covenant of Works which God formed with Adam when he was created has been discussed above under Ques. 12. The answer to Ques. 16 proceeds further to assert that this covenant was not made with Adam as a private person, but with him as the root and representative of all mankind. Hence not only himself, but all his posterity equally with himself, were concerned in its terms.

Adam's natural headship is the ground of his federal headship. If the question is, How, by what means, does it come to pass that every human being comes into the world with a depraved nature? the answer is that Adam and Eve, the natural root and origin of all men, corrupted their own nature, which corrupt nature is necessarily propagated to each new-born descendant by natural generation. If the question be, WHY, on what ground of justice, God brings this terrible curse of hereditary depravity upon each new-born soul before he has personally done either good or evil? the answer is that each one of us, being represented in the holy new-created Adam, had a far safer, fairer probation than we, any of us, could have had in our own persons after Adam's sin had corrupted the fountain from which we spring.

The angels had each his probation in his own person. But there is no Christ for fallen angels. Each angel who sinned remains hopelessly lost. Each angel which stood the first trial continues to keep his first estate. But since we fell in Adam, the representative of all men, we are saved in Christ, the second Adam, the representative of his own people, of his "sheep."

The representative principle is grounded both in nature and in Scripture. Children do everywhere inherit the good or evil consequences of their parents' lives. "The free will of the parent becomes the destiny of the child" (Hugh Miller). Witness the declaration attached to the Second Commandment (Ex. 20 : 5), the representative character of Christ the second Adam. He assumed the legal responsibility for our sins, and the reward of his righteousness is given to us. (See Rom. 5 : 12–21.)

The full penalty denounced upon Adam and Eve as the punishment of their apostasy has been continuously and rigorously inflicted on each of their descendants—death (Gen. 2 : 17) and pains of childbirth, a cursed earth, and the necessity of gaining our daily bread by the sweat of our brow (Gen. 3 : 16–19).

5th. THE ESTATE OF SIN INTO WHICH THAT ACT OF APOSTASY BROUGHT ALL MANKIND. Ques. 17, 18.

Q. 17. *Into what estate did the fall bring mankind?*

A. *The fall brought mankind into an estate of sin and misery.*

Q. 18. *Wherein consists the sinfulness of that estate whereinto man fell?*

A. *The sinfulness of that estate whereinto man fell, consists in the guilt of Adam's first sin, the want of original righteousness, and the corruption of his whole nature, which is commonly called* ORIGINAL SIN; *together with all actual transgressions which proceed from it.*

Sin is any want of conformity in (1) the actions, (2) the moral condition, and (3) the legal relations of a man with the law of God. But the sinful moral condition must precede, and is the source from which the evil actions must come. A universal fact must have a universal cause. As all men without exception begin to sin actively as soon as they arrive at moral agency, their inherited nature must be depraved, and the inherited depravity of nature must be the cause of that universal fact. This inherited depravity of nature, which comes to every man at birth and before he exercises sinful acts, is what is meant by the theological phrase "Original Sin," or the sin which is the fountain or origin of all other sin.

This original or birth sin, which comes to each of us at birth by natural generation, is (1) inflicted upon us as the just punishment of Adam's act of apostasy. It comes upon us as God's judgment upon "the guilt of Adam's first sin." (2) It is not merely a negative state—*i. e.* the loss of that original holiness or righteousness which

THE SIN AND MISERY OF MAN. 35

adorned the persons of our first parents when created. It does consist in this loss, but in addition it includes (3) the moral corruption of our whole nature.

This moral corruption of our whole nature involves (1) spiritual blindness of our minds (1 Cor. 2 : 14, 15 ; John 12 : 40); (2) hardening and moral perversion of our affections; (3) perversity of our wills. Hence our actions are morally corrupt. "There is none that doeth good, no, not one" (Ps. 14 : 3 ; Matt. 12 : 33–37). Even in the Christian there remains a "law in his members warring against the law of his mind, and bringing him into captivity to the law of sin which is in his members" (Rom. 7 : 23); "Both Jews and Gentiles are all under sin," "for all have sinned and come short of the glory of God;" "Therefore by the deeds of the law there shall no flesh be justified in his sight" (Rom. 3d chap.).

6th. THE ESTATE OF MISERY WHICH IS INSEPARABLE FROM THAT ESTATE OF SIN. Ques. 19.

Q. 19. *What is the misery of that estate whereinto man fell?*

A. *All mankind by their fall lost communion with God, are under his wrath and curse, and so made liable to all the miseries in this life, to death itself, and to the pains of hell for ever.*

All created rational spirits are so constituted that they can continue to exist in a holy and happy state only while living in immediate fellowship and active sympathy with the Father of all spirits. Sin at once cut man off from the possibility of this communion. (1) God is holy and righteously offended with us because we are sinners. Sin is that thing which God hateth, and he cannot look upon it with any degree of allowance. (2) We are alienated in our hearts from the holy God, and are full of a slavish fear of his just punishments.

Man, having been righteously cut off from this communion with God, instantaneously died (1) spiritually, (2) became mortal, so that before long his body inevitably dies. (3) Spiritual death, continued after the judgment, becomes eternal death, the second death.

The wrath and curse of God, which rests upon all men out of Christ in this world and in that which is to come, has none of the weakness of human passion, but is judicial, at once infinitely wise, just, and holy, and is inexpressibly terrible. It is the natural and necessary attitude which his absolutely righteous nature assumes in relation to our sins, and to us when unrepentant sinners. It is not only the greatest of all evils, but the immediate source of all other evils—afflicting the body and the soul in time and in eternity. It must last as long as unatoned and unrepented sin lasts. Since those who leave this life impenitent will never be brought to repentance, and will never be justified through the blood of Christ in the future state, it follows that their unending and accumulating sin must be accompanied with unending and ever-accumulating misery.

CALAMITY is suffering having, as far as known to us, no special relation to sin. Hence our Saviour forbids us to judge that great sufferers are therefore great sinners (Luke 13 : 1–5).

PENALTY is suffering inflicted upon sinners, and designed to satisfy the justice of God and to expiate the guilt of men. All suffering in this world irrespective of the work of Christ and of our relations to him is penal. And as long as the sin continues, and as long as

THE PLAN OF REDEMPTION. 37

its guilt is not expiated and the justice of God is not satisfied, so long will these penal sufferings be inflicted.

But in the case of all true believers in Christ the justice of God has been satisfied and the guilt of their sin has been expiated by his atoning death. Therefore, none of the sufferings of true believers in Christ are ever of the nature of punishment. They never express the wrath and curse of God. They are CHASTISEMENTS, and always express his love. CHASTISEMENTS are sufferings inflicted out of love to improve the character of the sufferer (Heb. 12 : 6–11).

E. GOD'S GRACIOUS METHOD OF REDEEMING MEN FROM THAT ESTATE OF SIN AND MISERY INTO WHICH THEY WERE BROUGHT BY THE APOSTASY OF ADAM. Ques. 20–38.

This includes (1) God's Plan of Redemption;
(2) The Redeemer and his Person;
(3) His Offices and Work;
(4) His Estates;
(5) The Application of Redemption by the Holy Ghost;
(6) The Benefits conferred by it in this Life;
(7) The Benefits conferred by it at Death;
(8) The Benefits conferred by it at the Resurrection.

1st. GOD'S PLAN OF REDEMPTION. Ques. 20.

Q. 20. *Did God leave all mankind to perish in the estate of sin and misery?*

A. *God, having out of his mere good pleasure, from all eternity, elected some to everlasting life, did enter into a covenant of grace, to deliver them out of the estate of sin and misery, and to bring them into an estate of salvation by a Redeemer.*

This includes—1st, The Motive;
2d, The Subjects;
3d, The Method of Redemption.

(1st) The motive was "his mere good pleasure"—*i. e.* his free and sovereign grace existing in his heart from all eternity with reference to those whom he has determined to save out of the mass of fallen mankind. Justice demands the punishment of the guilty. There is no alternative unless an adequate substitute is offered. Justice *must* be satisfied or injustice is done. But grace or unmerited favor to the ill-deserving sinner must necessarily be a matter wholly of God's sovereign discretion. All that we can say in view of its exercise, whether he chooses to save all sinners, many, few, or none, is, "Even so, Father, for so it seemed good in thy sight."

The most essential characteristic of the salvation of Christ is that it is entirely of grace from beginning to end. Men have no merit, either after or before they are united to Christ. On the contrary, they are always covered with ill desert. This is everywhere asserted in Scripture and implied in every single view of the mission and work of Christ and of the Holy Ghost (Rom. 3 : 23, 24; 5 : 15, 16; 11 : 6; Eph. 1 : 6, 7; 2 : 7; Tit. 2 : 11). That salvation is entirely of grace, that God might have justly passed by us and all other men, is felt and acknowledged by every true Christian. If this is not felt, Christ cannot be truly received as our Saviour.

(2d) The subjects of this redemption are those persons whom God has from all eternity elected of his sovereign good pleasure, out of the mass of fallen humanity, to everlasting life. This number is never said to be small, either absolutely or relatively. The promise to Abraham

THE COVENANT OF GRACE. 39

was that "his seed" (believers) should be multiplied "as the stars of the heaven, and as the sand which is upon the seashore." The strictest Calvinists believe that the number of the elect includes all who die in infancy, and that in the end it will embrace the vast majority of the human race.

This does not mean that Christ did not really die for all men, so that whosoever will believe on him shall have everlasting life. "For God so loved the world that he gave his only-begotten Son, that whosoever believeth in him should not perish, but have everlasting life" (John 3 : 16). He has suffered the penalty the law denounced on all human sinners, and so removed the legal obstacles to the salvation of every one who accepts Christ as his Saviour. Nevertheless, faith itself is the gift of God, and if any man truly believes, he knows that it was only because he was moved thereto by the Holy Ghost. Those whom God thus effectually moves are those whom he has, out of special love, elected to salvation and to all the means thereof from all eternity (John 6 : 37, 39 ; 10 : 26 ; Acts 13 : 48; Eph. 1 : 4–6). This also follows from the revealed fact that God's eternal decree determines whatsoever comes to pass. (See above, Ques. 7.) This works no injustice to those not elected. They will be only treated as they deserve. They have willfully sinned. Many of them have willfully rejected a freely and lovingly offered Christ (Rom. 9 : 19–23).

(3d) The method of redemption, or the Plan which God executes in redeeming sinners, is a "covenant." This, which is commonly called the "Covenant of Redemption," was formed in eternity between the several Persons of the Trinity, especially between the First and Second Persons. If God is an infinite and eternal intelligence, he must have had an eternal and all-comprehensive plan. If God consists of three distinct Persons, their plan must have been mutual; that is, it must have been of the nature of a covenant. A covenant implies parties and mutual conditions. The parties to the eternal Covenant of Redemption were Father, Son, and Holy Ghost.

The Father elected the beneficiaries, appointed the Son to take upon himself their nature, to assume and discharge all their legal responsibilities, and to merit for them eternal life and all the means thereof. He also appointed the Holy Ghost to apply and consummate this salvation in each elect person, and to dwell in the whole body of the elect as a whole. He promised the Son a body, all the providential conditions of his work, and the final salvation and glorification of his seed.

The Son voluntarily assumed the position to which he was appointed, and consecrated himself, in behalf of the elect, whose Head he became, to the dreadful humiliation and suffering involved.

The Holy Spirit voluntarily undertook his work of co-operating with Christ throughout his earthly life, and of applying his redemption after his ascension and session at the right hand of God (John 7 : 39; 14 : 16, 17; 16 : 7; Acts 2 : 33).

That such a Covenant of Redemption was formed before the world was is certain from what Christ says of his being sent into this world, of receiving a commandment as to the work he had to do from his Father, and from what he says of his sheep "as the gift and promise of his Father" (John 10 : 18; 5 : 23, 24, 30; 17 : 6, 24).

THE COVENANT OF GRACE. 41

The name "Covenant of Grace," as distinct from the "Covenant of Redemption," is commonly given to the gospel Covenant, which God offers to all men, and which he actually forms with all true believers. The "parties" to *this* covenant are God and believers. The "promise" is salvation, and all the means and conditions and stages thereof. The "condition" of this covenant is spiritual living faith—a faith which grasps, trusts in, and appropriates Christ in all his offices.

Christ is called the MEDIATOR of this covenant (Heb. 8 : 6; 9 : 15; 12 : 24), because it altogether rests on his meritorious work, and is effected through his ever-living agency as Mediator between God and man. He is also called the "Surety" of this covenant (Heb. 7 : 22), because he undertakes (endorses) for all his elect, engaging for them severally that they shall perform, and persevere in the performance of, all the conditions which the covenant requires of them.

The "faith" and "perseverance therein" of believers is not a "condition" of salvation in the sense that it possesses merit of itself. But it is the necessary instrument of our salvation, which the Holy Ghost provides and uses, whereby we receive and appropriate the righteousness of Christ and the gifts of the Holy Ghost, and whereby we recognize and are duly exercised by the various truths of God's Word and by the discipline of his Providence.

2d. THE REDEEMER AND HIS PERSON. Ques. 21, 22.

Q. 21. *Who is the Redeemer of God's elect?*

A. *The only Redeemer of God's elect is the Lord Jesus Christ, who being the eternal Son of God, became man,* and so was, and continueth to be, God and man, in two distinct natures, and one person for ever.

Q. 22. How did Christ, being the Son of God, become man?

A. Christ, the Son of God, became man, by taking to himself a true body and a reasonable soul, being conceived by the power of the Holy Ghost, in the womb of the Virgin Mary, and born of her, yet without sin.

These answers include—(1) The Incarnation; (2) The Person of Christ.

1st. The Incarnation is a great mystery which can be known only so far forth as it is revealed. Human speculations on the subject are of no value.

It implies, of course, the doctrine of the Trinity, which has been discussed above under Question 6. The eternal Son, the Second Person of the Godhead, is the Person incarnated. This was done by his voluntarily taking into his Person, in personal union with his divinity, the germs of a human soul and body. These human germs had a human mother, but no human father. They were conceived of the seed of the Virgin Mary by the power of the Holy Ghost (Rom. 1 : 3 ; Luke 1 : 35). This personal union of natures, once established, is to continue for ever. The human germs grew naturally for nine months in the womb of the Virgin, and after a natural birth his human nature underwent a natural growth until he attained complete manhood (Luke 2 : 52). After his resurrection and ascension and session at the right hand of the Father in heaven, this human nature has been endowed with powers and exalted to a state of honor and of glory beyond that of any other creature (Matt. 25 : 31–46 ; Rev. 20 : 11, 12 ; Rev. 1 : 10–18).

This union of two natures in Christ is in some few respects like the union of the material body and of the spiritual soul in one person in each of us. The soul is the person, not the body. Yet in conception the soul takes the germs of the body into that person as part of itself; separates from it and lays it down at death; and takes it back into its person for ever at the resurrection. So the Person of Christ is his eternal Godhead, which eternally exists as the Second Person of the Trinity. The humanity is taken into this union for ever. The bond is in this order: the eternal Son is united directly to the human soul, spirit to spirit, and through the human soul to the human body. At his death the break took place for three days between the human body of Christ and this human soul, and not between the human soul and his divine spirit.

2d. The Person of Christ. The same historical Person was born, increased in wisdom and in stature, hungered, thirsted, slept, ate, drank, wept, suffered, and died, loved, talked, obeyed, held social intercourse as a man, and prayed, and nevertheless is declared to be the almighty God, the everlasting Father, the Prince of Peace, commanding the elements, discerning the secrets of all hearts, breaking the bands of the grave, and, sitting upon the right hand of God, assuming the reins of universal empire. He is evidently in all situations one and the same Person. Yet the divine and human natures are not mixed, but remain pure and entire. The same Person is and does all that is proper either to God or man. His human nature is finite, existing under the limits of time and space. His divine nature is eternal and omnipresent. His human nature is now locally present only in heaven. Nevertheless, he is virtually present to all his people with his sympathy, knowledge, assistance, and comfort as a man and brother who has suffered as they have, through his divine nature and through the co-operation of the Holy Ghost.

God is said to have purchased the Church with his own blood, and the Lord of glory is said to have been crucified (Acts 20 : 28; 1 Cor. 2 : 8), because the one Person who is God was also man. The Son of man is said to have been in heaven and earth at the same time (John 3 : 13), because the one Person who is man was also God.

In all mediatorial actions as prophet, priest, and king the attributes of both the divine and human natures were in exercise as the properties of the one mediatorial Person.

3d. HIS OFFICES AND WORK. Ques. 23–26.

Q. 23. *What offices doth Christ execute as our Redeemer?*

A. *Christ, as our Redeemer, executeth the offices of a prophet, of a priest, and of a king, both in his estate of humiliation and exaltation.*

The word "office" is used in two senses. The more common sense is that of a legally defined position to which a certain work (*munus*) is assigned. The other sense is that of some particular part or function involved in the performance of the work. Thus to the office or *munus* of President of the United States many particular offices or functions are attached, as those of executing the laws, concurring with the two houses of Congress in making the laws, appointing subordinate officers to carry on the details of the administration, etc. etc.

THE MEDIATORIAL OFFICE OF CHRIST. 45

Thus in the fuller sense Christ as our Redeemer holds only one indivisible office, that of the only Mediator between man and God. But this single indivisible office embraces three classes of functions, which should be distinguished in idea, although they are really inseparable in fact; these are the functions of prophet, priest, and king. Like the functions of enervation, of circulation of the blood, and of breathing the air, these mutually coexist and act together in all the mediatorial activities of our Lord. He always teaches as a Royal Priest. He was a Royal Prophet even when he hung upon the tree. He ever continues a teaching and atoning Prophetical Priest while he sits and reigns from his throne as King.

It is clearly necessary that the Mediator between God and man should be both divine and human in order to discharge the functions of that office.

(1st) He must be God—(*a*) that he might be independent of either party to be reconciled, and so *make the peace;* (*b*) that he might originate the revelation of God to man; (*c*) that, being personally above the demands of law and of infinite dignity, he might be put in our law-place, render an obedience he did not owe for himself, and by one death atone for the sins of all his people, and for them merit an eternal reward; (*d*) that he might be King over all things for his Church.

(2d) It is no less clear that he must be man—(*a*) that as the second Adam he might represent man; (*b*) that he might be made under the law, render obedience, suffer the penalty of sin for men, and be tempted in all things like us, sin excepted; (*c*) that he might sympathize as a merciful and faithful High Priest (Heb. 2: 17, 18; 4: 15, 16); (*d*) that he might in his glorified humanity be the Head of the Church to whom all his people "are predestined to be conformed" (Rom. 8 : 29).

(1st.) HIS OFFICE AS PROPHET. Ques. 24.

Q. 24. *How doth Christ execute the office of a prophet?*

A. *Christ executeth the office of a prophet, in revealing to us by his Word and Spirit, the will of God for our salvation.*

A prophet is one qualified and authorized to speak for God to men. Moses was prophet for his brother Aaron (Ex. 7 : 1). The foretelling future events is only one part, and that not the most characteristic or important, of the function of a prophet.

Christ executed the office of a Prophet as the WORD OF GOD in three grand stages: (*a*) before his incarnation; (*b*) after his incarnation during the present dispensation; (*c*) throughout eternity in glory.

He has executed it (1) *immediately* in his own Person —(*a*) on earth, (*b*) in heaven; (2) *mediately*—(*a*) through the Holy Ghost by inspiration of the prophets and apostles, and by the spiritual illumination of all his people; (*b*) hence through the inspired Scriptures; (*c*) through the officers of his Church, as qualified with supernatural gifts as the apostles, or with only natural gifts and ordinary graces as pastors and teachers.

He executes the functions of a divine Prophet in our behalf both (*a*) externally, as through his Word and works, and (*b*) internally, by means of the spiritual illumination of our hearts. He is not only *a* prophet, but *the* Prophet. For as God he alone knows the deep things of God, and can adequately and authoritatively speak for him. He is the original Fountain of all divine knowledge among

THE MEDIATORIAL OFFICE OF CHRIST. 47

men, the eternal WORD and IMAGE of God (John 3 : 11), the Prophet of prophets, the Teacher of teachers.

He is called, in the Old Testament, Counsellor (Isa. 9 : 6), Interpreter (Job 33 : 23), Witness (Isa. 55 : 4). In the New Testament he is asserted to have taught through the prophets of the Old Testament (1 Pet. 1 : 11 ; Luke 24 : 27. Comp. Deut. 18 : 15 with Acts 3 : 22 ; 7 : 37).

(2d.) HIS OFFICE AS A PRIEST. Ques. 25.

Q. *How doth Christ execute the office of a priest?*

A. *Christ executeth the office of a priest, in his once offering up of himself a sacrifice to satisfy divine justice, and reconcile us to God, and in making continual intercession for us.*

This involves four points: (1) What is a priest? (2) Christ was a real Priest. (3) He offered himself on the cross a sacrifice for our sins to satisfy the justice of God. (4) He ever lives to make intercession for us.

(1) A priest must be (*a*) a man, taken from among men to represent them ; (*b*) he must be appointed and authorized by God; (*c*) holy, morally pure, and consecrated to God (Lev. 21 : 6, 8); (*d*) he must have a right to approach immediately into the presence of God, with assurance of his favor ; (*e*) he must have the right to offer sacrifices to God and to make intercession in behalf of those represented by him (Heb. 5 : 1–6 ; Num. 16 : 5 ; Lev. 16 : 3, 7, 12, 15).

(2) Christ was a real and true Priest. (*a*) He was a man taken from among men to represent them (Heb. 2 : 16, 17 ; 4 : 15). (*b*) He was chosen by God (Heb. 5 : 5, 6). (*c*) He was perfectly holy (Luke 1 : 35 ; Heb. 7 : 26). (*d*) He had an absolute right of immediate access to God, and influence with him (John 17 : 26 ; 11 : 42 ; Heb. 1 : 3). (*e*)

He performed perfectly and absolutely all the functions of a priest (Eph. 5 : 2 ; Heb. 9 : 26 ; 10 : 11, 12 ; 1 John 2 : 1 ; Rom. 8 : 34).

Indeed, Christ is the *only* real Priest. Aaron and his sons were only types or shadows of Christ, as the paper dollar promising to pay is the shadow of the real gold dollar, which really pays. Christ and his sacrifice was the substance. He really did what they and their sacrifices merely symbolized (Heb. 9 : 10–12 ; 10 : 1 ; Col. 2 : 17).

(3) Christ offered himself on the cross a sacrifice for our sins to satisfy the justice of God.

The victims of the Jewish bloody sacrifices suffered the penalty of the law (death) in the stead of those in whose behalf they were offered. (*a*) They were offered on the occasion of sin, and by or on behalf of the sinner (Lev. 4 : 1–6, 13–16). (*b*) The victims must be perfect of their kind (Lev. 22 : 20–27 ; Ex. 22 : 30). (*c*) The sinner, or the priest representing the sinful people, laid hands on the head of the victim, confessing sin. "Laying on of hands" in Scripture always means transfer of something (Lev. 1 : 4 ; 3 : 2 ; 4 : 4 ; 16 : 21 ; 2 Chron. 29 : 23). (*d*) The victim, although perfect in itself, is after the laying on of hands called "sin" and "guilt" (Lev. 4 : 3 ; 5 : 6). (*e*) The victim was then slain in the sinner's stead ; "accepted for him to make atonement for him," "for it is the blood that maketh atonement for the soul" (Lev. 4 chap.; 17 : 11). (*f*) The blood was then sprinkled either on the horns of the altar or on the mercy-seat within the veil (Lev. 4 : 5, etc.). Thus the sin *was covered*, the Old-Testament word for expiation by blood or the satisfaction of justice, and hence God propitiated (Rom. 4 : 7). (*g*) The invariable effect of the sacrifice

THE MEDIATORIAL OFFICE OF CHRIST. 49

and of this application of the blood was forgiveness (Lev. 4 : 20–31 ; 5 : 10, 13, 16, 18 ; 6 : 7 ; Heb. 2 : 17).

Christ was at once the Priest and the Victim. "He offered himself without spot to God;" "he was offered to bear the sins of many" (Heb. 9 : 14, 28); "The Lord hath laid on him the iniquity of us all;" "He was wounded for our transgressions, he was bruised for our iniquities; the chastisement of our peace was upon him, and with his stripes we are healed" (Isa. 53 : 4–6); "It was not possible that the blood of bulls and of goats should take away sins. . . . By the which will we are sanctified through the offering of the body of Jesus Christ once for all" (Heb. 10 : 4, 10). Hence he "is the propitiation for our sins" (1 John 2 : 2), for " he hath redeemed us from the curse of the law, being made a curse for us " (Gal. 3 : 13); " Forasmuch as ye know that ye were not redeemed with corruptible things, as silver and gold, . . . but with the precious blood of Christ, as of a lamb without blemish and without spot" (1 Pet. 1 : 18, 19); God "made Him to be sin for us, who knew no sin, that we might be made the righteousness of God in him" (2 Cor. 5 : 21).

The "justice of God" as the Judge and Moral Governor of the universe of men and of angels "was satisfied," because the just sentence of death which he had pronounced upon our sins was executed upon the person of our substitute Jesus Christ, who had voluntarily assumed our place under the law.

(4) Christ ever lives to make intercession for us (Heb. 7 : 25 ; Rom. 8 : 34). Christ is an ever-living, perpetual Priest. He has a personal experience of all our trials and a fellow-feeling for our infirmities (Heb. 2 : 17, 18).

He is also a royal Priest. He intercedes for us on the throne (Zech. 6 : 13), from which he sends the Holy Spirit, and orders all events in all worlds for the good of his people (Acts 2 : 33; Matt. 28 : 18; Heb. 10 : 12, 13).

This intercession of our Lord as a royal Priest is one absolutely essential part of his work as Mediator. It was necessary for him not only to open up a way of possible salvation, but actually to accomplish the salvation of each one of those given to him by the Father, and actually to bring them to the Father at last (John 17 : 12; Eph. 2 : 18; 3 : 12). The communion of his people with the Father will ever be sustained through him as mediatorial Priest (Ps. 110 : 4; Rev. 7 : 17).

The one perfect specimen of our Lord's mediatorial intercession recorded for our comfort is the seventeenth chapter of John.

3d. HIS OFFICE AS KING. Ques. 26.

Q. 26. *How doth Christ execute the office of a king?*

A. *Christ executeth the office of a king, in his subduing us to himself, in ruling and defending us, and in restraining and conquering all his and our enemies.*

His mediatorial kingship differs from that royal authority which belongs to him as Second Person of the Godhead, (1) because it is *given* to him by the Father as the reward of his obedience and suffering (Phil. 2 : 6–11); (2) because the object and design of his mediatorial kingship is not general, but has special reference to his redeemed Church (Eph. 1 : 22, 23). The person possessing this mediatorial power is the entire God-man.

THE KINGLY OFFICE OF CHRIST. 51

This royal power belongs to Christ now, and it extends (1) over his own Church, which is in a special sense his kingdom (Acts 2 : 29–36); (2) over the whole universe (Eph. 1 : 17–23; Matt. 28 : 18).

He exercises it, *first*, in effectually calling out of the world a people for himself, and in establishing his kingdom in their hearts; *second*, in establishing that kingdom as a community of believers, in giving to them a constitution, laws, and officers, and in presiding over their administration and service; *thirdly*, in bestowing saving grace upon his elect, and dispensing his Spirit as the source of all spiritual life and blessedness; *fourthly*, in dispensing the general providential government of the world and of all its affairs so as to cause all things to work together for the good of his people and for the advancement of his kingdom and glory; *fifthly*, in his restraining and conquering all the enemies of his kingdom; and *sixthly*, in his final judgment of the world and of all its inhabitants, and the punishment of his enemies and the rewarding of his friends.

Christ will for ever continue the Head and King of his own Church. The redeemed will never be separated from their Redeemer. But his *mediatorial headship as the God-man* over the universe he will, after the final judgment and consummation, give up to the Father, that God may be all and in all (1 Cor. 15 : 24–28). Christ's mediatorial kingdom over the universe, administered *providentially*, is called his KINGDOM OF POWER. His kingdom over his own Church, administered *spiritually*, is called his KINGDOM OF GRACE. His gracious kingdom when consummated hereafter will constitute his KINGDOM OF GLORY.

4th. THE REDEEMER: HIS ESTATES. Ques. 27, 28.

Q. 27. *Wherein did Christ's humiliation consist?*

A. *Christ's humiliation consisted in his being born, and that in a low condition, made under the law, undergoing the miseries of this life, the wrath of God, and the cursed death of the cross; in being buried, and continuing under the power of death for a time.*

The HUMILIATION began with his being born, and ended with his death and the passage of his soul into the invisible or spirit world.

(1st) "In his being born, and that in a low condition." It was an act of infinite condescension upon the part of the Second Person of the glorious Trinity, and of transcendent and permanent interest to the whole intelligent creation, that all the fullness of the Godhead should be contained in him *bodily*, and so revealed under the limitations of a finite nature. For it is only thus that the infinite One can be "seen and known," "tested and handled," and that of "his fullness" we may all receive, and "grace for grace" (John 1:16, 18: 1 John 1:1).

(2d) In his being "made under the law," and rendering perfect obedience to it. The law lays its claims upon persons. But the Person of Christ was eternal and divine. Personally, he was the Lawgiver, and not under any obligation of obedience. His supreme perfections are spontaneous, and are a law to all the dependent universe. The law was conformed to him, not he to the law.

But when he undertook the office of Mediator he voluntarily assumed, as the second Adam, all the legal responsibilities of his people. By his lifelong suffering and death Christ endured in our stead the punishment

THE HUMILIATION OF CHRIST. 53

due to our sins. By his lifelong obedience, even unto death, he merited for us the favor of God and eternal life, a happy and glorious immortality, and all the means thereof, and so purchased for us an everlasting inheritance in the kingdom of heaven.

Christ was therefore "made under the law" (Gal. 4: 4, 5)—(*a*) not as a rule of righteousness, but as a condition of blessedness (to us), "to redeem them that were under the law, that we might receive the adoption of sons;" (*b*) not for himself, but officially as our Substitute; (*c*) his whole obedience to that law was vicarious, in the stead of our obedience. "By the obedience of one shall many be made righteous" (Rom. 5 : 19).

(3d) "In his undergoing the miseries of this life, the wrath of God, and the cursed death of the cross." Personally in his own character he was always God's "beloved Son, in whom he was well pleased." But as a vicarious sacrifice in our stead, our sins and their punishment were borne by him, and God's wrath for our sins poured out upon him, he being "made a curse."

The essence of the penalty vicariously borne by Christ was "the wrath of God." The incidents of it were "the miseries of this life." The culmination of it was "the cursed death of the cross" (Gen. 2 : 17; Heb. 9 : 22).

(4th) In "his being buried, and continuing under the power of death for a time." This is the consummation and conclusion of his vicarious death. In the Apostles' Creed, which is adopted by all the churches, this is expressed by the phrase, "He descended into hell"—*i. e.* *Hades*, the spirit-world. This word and also the Hebrew word *sheol* mean the world where the disembodied spirits of men are gathered after death and before the resurrection. The wicked were there in chains and darkness, reserved unto the judgment of the last day (Jude 6). The righteous were there holy and happy, waiting for the consummation of their salvation in the resurrection of their bodies. The part of Hades in which the good were collected was called " Abraham's bosom " and " Paradise " (Luke 16 : 22 ; 23 : 43). The soul of Christ, still united to his divinity, leaving his body in the grave, immediately upon his death went to Paradise, where the spirits of all good men were gathered. And in going there he made it bright and glorious by his presence. Where Christ is, *there* is heaven.

Q. 28. *Wherein consisteth Christ's exaltation?*

A. *Christ's exaltation consisteth in his rising again from the dead on the third day, in ascending up into heaven, in sitting at the right hand of God the Father, and in coming to judge the world at the last day.*

(1) " In his rising again from the dead on the third day." This stupendous fact is the most certain and the most surely proved event in ancient history. It was a plain, simple fact, capable of the most thorough examination and certain demonstration. The single points are that Christ was really dead on Friday, and that he was really alive again in the body on Sunday and afterward. Both points were proved by the strictest evidence. His body both before and afterward was *seen and handled* over and over again by many different persons. Thomas examined the marks of its identity critically, and then exclaimed, " My Lord and my God !"

It was (*a*) predicted in the Old Testament. (Compare Ps. 16 : 10 ; Acts 2 : 24–31.) (*b*) Christ himself predicted it (Matt. 20 : 18, 19 ; John 10 : 17, 18). (*c*) It

THE EXALTATION OF CHRIST. 55

was witnessed to by the eleven apostles (Acts 1 : 3). (*d*) It was testified to by Paul as an independent witness (1 Cor. 15 : 8 ; Gal. 1 : 12 ; Acts 9 : 3–8). (*e*) He was seen by the five hundred brethren at once (1 Cor. 15 : 6). (*f*) The miracles wrought by the apostles attested the fact (Heb. 2 : 4). (*g*) Also the witness of the Holy Ghost (Acts 5 : 32). (*h*) Also the change of the Sabbath from the seventh to the first day of the week.

The importance of this great fact is proved, (*a*) because it proved him to be the Son of God and authenticates all his claims. (*b*) It was a public acceptance by his Father of his mediatorial work in our behalf. (*c*) Henceforth we have an ever-living Saviour at the right hand of power (Rom. 8 : 34). (*d*) His resurrection secures ours (1 Cor. 6 : 15 ; 15 : 49 ; Phil. 3 : 21).

(2) " In ascending up into heaven." This took place forty days after his resurrection, in the presence of the eleven apostles and probably other friends. He ascended in his complete Person as God-man, body and spirit, as our Mediator, triumphing over his enemies and giving gifts to his friends (Eph. 4 : 8–12), to complete his mediatorial work as the forerunner of his people, and to fill the universe with his glory (John 17 : 23 ; Heb. 6 : 20 ; Eph. 4 : 10).

(3) " In his sitting at the right hand of the Father." This denotes the official exaltation of the God-man as Mediator to supreme glory, felicity, and dominion over every name that is named. There he intercedes for his people as a priest upon a throne (Zech. 6 : 13), and from thence he effectually applies to his people, by his Spirit, that salvation which he had previously achieved for them in the days of his humiliation (Ps. 16 : 11 ; 110 : 1 ;

Dan. 7 : 13, 14; Matt. 26 : 64; Mark 16 : 19; John 5 : 22; Rom. 8 : 34; Eph. 1 : 20, 22; Phil. 2 : 9-11; Col. 3 : 1; Heb. 1 : 3, 4; 2 : 9; 10 : 12; 1 Pet. 3 : 22; Rev. 5 : 6).

(4) "In his coming to judge the world at the last day." The time of this general judgment is entirely unknown to men. But it is revealed that it will come suddenly at last like a thief in the night, and that it will occur immediately upon the second advent of Christ and the general resurrection of all the dead.

God has appointed this day of general judgment, and he has committed it into the hands of the God-man as Mediator. He that was rejected of men, tried and condemned by Pilate, shall have before him on trial the whole human family without exception.

The good shall be gathered on his right, the evil upon his left. The thoughts of all hearts shall be revealed, and every secret feeling of the soul and all words and actions shall be brought up for trial.

The books shall be opened—the book of record, in which all the history of our lives is written, and the Book of Life, in which the names of all those who are chosen and who have been united to Christ by a living faith, are written.

Every one is to be judged justly in view of the real state of their hearts and motives, and in view of their respective amount of knowledge of God's will. The heathen who sinned without the law will be judged without the law. He who has sinned knowing not his Lord's will, will be beaten with few stripes. They who have sinned under the light of the gospel "will have no cloak for their sin." It will be better for Sodom and Go-

THE APPLICATION OF REDEMPTION. 57

morrah in the day of judgment than for us if we neglect this great salvation.

Then will the God-man, who once wore a crown of thorns, pronounce final sentence upon each soul: "Come, ye blessed of my Father, inherit the kingdom prepared for you from the foundation of the world;" or, "Depart from me, ye cursed, into everlasting fire, prepared for the devil and his angels" (Matt. 25 : 31–46; 2 Thess. 1 : 7–10; Rom. 2 : 6–16; Matt. 13 : 37–45; Mark 13 : 32–37; Rev. 22 : 20).

5th. THE APPLICATION OF REDEMPTION. Ques. 29–31.

THE AGENT.

Q. 29. *How are we made partakers of the redemption purchased by Christ?*

A. *We are made partakers of the redemption purchased by Christ, by the effectual application of it to us by the Holy Spirit.*

The Scriptures teach that men are by nature spiritually dead in trespasses and sins—that we cannot turn from sin unto God except we are first drawn by God (Ps. 51 : 5; Job 14 : 4; Eph. 4 : 18; Rom. 8 : 7, 8; John 6 : 44; Rev. 3 : 17). The salvation, therefore, which Christ has wrought out for us must be applied to us by the mighty power of God. The work of the Holy Spirit *in* us is just as essential as the work of Christ *for* us. And in the first instance we are no more able to co-operate in the work of the Spirit applying redemption than we are able to co-operate with the atoning work of Christ meritoriously effecting redemption.

This is rendered certain by what the Scriptures clearly teach: 1st, As to man's natural state as a sinner. He is declared to be spiritually—that is, as to spiritual objects and interests—"dead," "blind," "insensible," "helpless or impotent" (1 Cor. 2 : 14; 2 Cor. 4 : 4; Eph. 4 : 18; Col. 2 : 13; 2 Tim. 2 : 26; Matt. 12 : 33–35). 2d. It is proved by what the Scriptures teach as to the nature of the Spirit's work in the first steps of his application of the redemption purchased by Christ. It is called "a new birth," "a quickening," "a begetting," "a new creation" (John 3 : 3, 5–7; 1 John 5 : 18; Eph. 2 : 1, 5, 10; 4 : 23). In all these respects the life-giving act of God must precede the act of the creature. He "creates," "begets," "quickens," and then we live and act in a manner corresponding to the new life. The order is as follows: The soul is dead; God quickens it. The soul repents and believes; it is then justified freely through faith in the blood of Christ. Then it enters upon a course of holy obedience, in which the Holy Spirit continually sustains, prompts, and guides it; thus it grows in grace continually, being progressively more and more sanctified inwardly, and outwardly enabled more and more to resist evil and conform to the example and commandments of Christ.

This is the special office-work of the Holy Ghost, the Third Person of the glorious Trinity.

Christ promised to send the Holy Spirit, and that he should testify of Christ and receive of Christ, and show it unto us (John 15 : 26 ; 16 : 7–14). When Christ ascended and sat down at the right hand of God, he fulfilled his promise and sent the Holy Spirit in his fullness to his Church (John 7 : 39; Acts 2 : 32, 33). Christ has given us the Spirit to abide with us for ever as "another Advocate:" this is the same term translated Advocate

EFFECTUAL CALLING. 59

when applied to Christ (1 John 2 : 1; compare John 14 : 16, 26; 15 : 26; 16 : 7–9).

Regeneration, sanctification, and all the operations of grace in the hearts of men are referred to the Holy Ghost (John 6 : 63; Rom. 8 : 9, 11, 14, 16, 26; 1 Cor. 12 : 13; Gal. 4 : 6, 7; Eph. 2 : 18). Hence in the Nicene Creed, received by all the churches, the Holy Ghost is called "THE LORD, THE GIVER OF LIFE."

Q. 30. *How doth the Spirit apply to us the redemption purchased by Christ?*

A. *The Spirit applieth to us the redemption purchased by Christ, by working faith in us and thereby uniting us to Christ in our effectual calling.*

Q. 31. *What is effectual calling?*

A. *Effectual calling is the work of God's Spirit, whereby, convincing us of our sin and misery, enlightening our minds in the knowledge of Christ, and renewing our wills, he doth persuade and enable us to embrace Jesus Christ, freely offered to us in the gospel.*

The Scriptures expressly teach that there are two calls to salvation—the one outward by the Word, the other inward by the Spirit. Of the subjects of the first call it is said, "Many are called, but few are chosen" (Matt. 22 : 14). Of the subjects of the other call it is said, "Whom he called, them he also justified" (Rom. 8 : 30; compare Prov. 1 : 24 and John 6 : 45).

(1) The outward call of the Word is divinely appointed, and is, under all ordinary conditions, a necessary means of salvation. The established order is—salvation cometh by faith, faith cometh by hearing, and hearing by the Word of God (Rom. 10 : 13–17; Mark 16 : 15, 16).

This outward call of the Word consists (*a*) of a statement of the plan and conditions of salvation through Jesus Christ. (*b*) A command to repent and believe on Christ. (*c*) An exhibition of the motives which should naturally dispose men to accept and obey the gospel. (*d*) A promise of salvation in case we do repent and believe.

This outward call is in absolute good faith; without possible exception, whosoever does repent and believe shall be saved; and it is intended to be addressed to all men, to every creature, of every nation, of all times, to the end of the world (Mark 16 : 15, 16 ; Rev. 22 : 16, 17).

(2) But there is also an inward spiritual call, distinct from that of the Word. This is proved (*a*) from the fact that the Scriptures teach that man by nature is spiritually "dead" and "blind" and impotent. In order that the blind shall see, two things are necessary : their eyes must be opened, and they must have light. The outward call supplies the light. The inward call opens the eye. (*b*) The Scriptures distinguish between the Spirit's influence and that of the Word alone (1 Cor. 2 : 14, 15 ; 3 : 6 ; 1 Thess. 1 : 5, 6). (*c*) A spiritual influence is said to be necessary to dispose and enable men to receive the truth (John 6 : 45 ; Acts 16 : 14 ; Eph. 1 : 17). (*d*) All that is good in man is referred to God as its author (Eph. 2 : 8 ; Phil. 2 : 13 ; 2 Tim. 2 : 25 ; Heb. 13 : 21). (*e*) The working of the Spirit in the heart of the new-born Christian is represented as far more direct and powerful than the mere moral influence of the truth on the natural understanding and affections (Eph. 1 : 19 ; 3 : 7 ; 2 : 1, 8). (*f*) The effects of this inward call of the Holy Ghost are far more profound and lasting than any mere moral

influence of the external call. It is declared to be a "new birth," "a begetting," "a quickening from death to life," "a new creation." The subjects of it are "newborn babes," and "new creatures," and "God's workmanship," and "alive from the dead."

There are certain influences of the Holy Spirit which in a greater or less degree extend to all men. These influences are simply moral, acting on the soul through the truth and exciting its natural affections and powers. They are more or less influential in modifying conduct, but they are habitually resisted by the souls of men as long as they remain unregenerate. This is proved (*a*) from the fact that the Scriptures affirm that they are resisted; (*b*) from the fact that anterior to regeneration every Christian is conscious of having resisted such spiritual influences. The same we observe to be true in the history of many unregenerate men.

But the power used by the Holy Ghost in our effectual calling is always efficacious. Its effect is called Regeneration or the New Birth. It is the exercise of the mighty power of God directly upon the soul, quickening it to a new spiritual life. It is a single act of God the Holy Ghost. The effect, once produced, is preserved for ever by the continued indwelling of the Holy Ghost in our hearts. The change wrought affects the whole soul, the intellect, the affections, and will, and all their faculties (John 17:3; 1 Cor. 2:12, 13; 4:5; 2 Cor. 4:6; Eph. 1:18; 1 John 4:7; 5:20; Heb. 4:12).

REGENERATION is the work of God. It changes the character of the soul. It is below consciousness. CONVERSION is the act of the soul itself—the *first* act of the soul in turning from sin unto God, immediately consequent upon regeneration. It is always a matter of consciousness, and is the commencement of a course of progressive growth in the divine life, which goes on until we attain the complete stature of perfect manhood in Christ.

REGENERATION is the act of God, who begets. CONVERSION is the first vital act of the newly-begotten soul. Sanctification is the growth of the soul toward maturity.

6th. THE BENEFITS CONFERRED BY THIS REDEMPTION IN THIS LIFE TO ALL THOSE WHO ARE EFFECTUALLY CALLED. Ques. 32–36.

Q. 32. *What benefits do they who are effectually called partake of in this life?*

A. *They that are effectually called do in this life partake of justification, adoption, sanctification, and the several benefits, which, in this life, do either accompany or flow from them.*

Here we have enumerated four classes of benefits: (1) Justification; (2) Adoption; (3) Sanctification; (4) The several benefits which, in this life, do either accompany or flow from the three first enumerated.

(1) JUSTIFICATION. Ques. 33.

Q. 33. *What is Justification?*

A. *Justification is an act of God's free grace, wherein he pardoneth all our sins, and accepteth us as righteous in his sight, only for the righteousness of Christ imputed to us, and received by faith alone.*

(*a*) JUSTIFICATION is an "act." That is, it is accomplished perfectly and finished at once. It is not a progressive work.

JUSTIFICATION. 63

(*b*) It is a *forensic* act of God as Supreme Judge. It is neither an act of power, producing an effect by the exercise of irresistible energy, nor is it an act of sovereign prerogative in the exercise of unconditional right of will. It is a judicial act, wherein God as judge pronounces the judgment of the law in view of *all* the facts of the case—*namely*, that in view of the righteousness of Christ the believer is regarded and treated as one in whose behalf all the claims of the law are completely satisfied.

(*c*) It is an act wherein God "pardoneth all our sins." The fact being that we are personally sinners and in ourselves considered deserve the penalty, justification must include "pardon." But it is not mere pardon. Because [1] "pardon" is the act of a sovereign waiving the execution of the law; while "justification" is the act of a judge pronouncing the law to be satisfied. [2] "Pardon" is granted in the absence of all "satisfaction;" while justification is possible only after a "satisfaction" for the sin has been made. [3] "Pardon" merely releases from the obligation to suffer the penalty; while "justification" also restores to favor and to the full status of society.

(*d*) Hence JUSTIFICATION is an act wherein God "pardoneth all our sins" because he has "accepted us as righteous in his sight." A man is righteous when he is completely conformed to the law. If he is personally conformed in his heart and life to the law as a standard or measure of character, then he is no sinner, but perfectly holy. If he is perfectly conformed to the law as a covenant of salvation, he is righteous, whether the law as covenant has been fulfilled by the person himself or by his accepted and competent substitute. In our case we personally are sinners. But our Lord Jesus Christ by his holy suffering in our stead has satisfied the penalty of the law, and by his holy obedience in our stead has satisfied the precepts of the law. Upon the basis of that satisfaction we are pronounced righteous; which is the same as pronouncing the law to be satisfied in respect to all its demands upon us as a covenant of salvation.

(e) He "accepteth us as righteous in his sight only for the righteousness of Christ." This righteousness of Christ comprehends all that he did in the way of obedience or of suffering in our stead while on earth. No other being than the God-man could have thus acted in our stead. It was only in human nature that the demands of the law upon mankind could be met and satisfied. But it was only a divine Person, who is himself the law to all others, and is himself under no law exterior to his own will, who can render in the stead of another a free obedience which he does not owe for himself.

(f) And this "righteousness of Christ" is made the meritorious ground of our being judiciously pronounced to be righteous (i. e. that all the demands which the law as a covenant of life makes upon us are satisfied), because of two facts: [1] Because that the righteousness of Christ "is imputed to us;" and [2] because it is "received by us by faith alone."

[1] To impute sin to any one is to charge it as a ground of punishment. It may be a man's own sin (Ps. 32:2), or it may the sin of others—i. e. not their personal blameworthiness, but their guilt or obligation to punishment. Thus our sins are said to have been laid upon and punished in Christ (Isa. 53:6, 12; Gal. 3:13; Heb. 9:28; 1 Pet. 2:24).

JUSTIFICATION. 65

[2] To impute righteousness is to credit it as the ground of justification or of reward. Thus the rewardableness of Christ's meritorious work is credited to the believer, so that all the covenanted rewards of a perfect righteousness henceforth lawfully belong to him (Rom. 4 : 4–8 ; 2 Cor. 5 : 19–21).

(*g*) This righteousness of Christ is imputed only to one who believes, and so it is received and self-appropriated only by faith. This justifying or saving faith has no merit in itself. It is only the hand or instrument by which we lay hold of Christ. It includes trust. It is faith *in* or *on* Christ (Gal. 2 : 16 ; Acts 16 : 31). This faith is the "gift of God" (Eph. 2 : 8); it never exists alone, but is always accompanied with love, and bears holy fruit in the life. But it alone, and no other grace, is the instrument of uniting us to Christ, and so of effecting our justification.

(*h*) Justification is therefore "an act of God's *free grace.*" It is absolutely sovereign and pre-eminently gratuitous, in that Christ is given to assume our place, and in that his righteousness is allowed to count in the stead of ours. At the same time, after this substitution is once sovereignly admitted justification is strictly judicial, being perfectly conformed to law and justice, since Christ as our Substitute has literally and completely fulfilled all the requirements of the law, both commandments and penalties.

Calvin says, in his *Institutes*, b. 3, chap. 11, § 2 : "A man will be justified by faith when, excluded from the righteousness of works, he by faith lays hold of the righteousness of Christ, and, clothed in it, appears in the sight of God, not as a sinner, but as righteous."

(2) ADOPTION. Ques. 34.

Q. 34. *What is Adoption?*

A. *Adoption is an act of God's free grace, whereby we are received into the number, and have a right to all the privileges of the sons of God.*

The instant a believer is united to Christ by faith, there is accomplished in him simultaneously and inseparably *two* things: (a) A total change of relation to God and to the law as a covenant of life; (b) a change in his inward spiritual nature. The change of *relation* is effected by justification, the change of *nature* by regeneration. REGENERATION is an act of God, giving a new life, the principle of a new spiritual character. The first exercise of a new-born soul thus regenerated is FAITH. Upon the exercise of faith, or a trusting embrace of the person and work of Christ, God immediately *justifies* the believer, freeing him from condemnation and receiving him into favor. SANCTIFICATION is the progressive growth toward perfect maturity of the new life implanted in regeneration. ADOPTION presents the new creature in his new relations. Justification effects a change of relations. Regeneration and sanctification affect only moral inherent states of the soul. Adoption includes both. It sets forth in one comprehensive view the new creature in his new relations.

Sonship includes (a) derivation of nature (2 Pet. 1 : 4; John 1 : 13); (b) the bearing of the divine image or likeness (Col. 3 : 10; Rom. 8 : 29; 2 Cor. 3 : 18); (c) the bearing the Father's name (1 John 3 : 1; Rev. 2 : 17; 3 : 12); (d) the being the objects of his peculiar love (John 17 : 23; Rom. 5 : 5–8); (e) the indwelling of the "Spirit of his Son," the "Spirit of Adoption" (Rom.

SANCTIFICATION. 67

8 : 15-21; Gal. 4 : 6; 5 : 1; 1 Pet. 1 : 14; Heb. 2 : 15; 10 : 19, 22); (*f*) present protection, consolation, and provision (Luke 12 : 27-32; John 14 : 18; 1 Cor. 3 : 21-23; 2 Cor. 1 : 4); (*g*) fatherly chastisement for our good (Ps. 51 : 11, 12; Heb. 12 : 5-11); (*h*) heirship in relation to God and joint heirship with Christ (Rom. 8 : 17; James 2 : 5; 1 Pet. 1 : 4; 5 : 4).

(3) SANCTIFICATION. Ques. 35.

Q. 35. *What is Sanctification?*

A. *Sanctification is the work of God's free grace, whereby we are renewed in the whole man after the image of God, and are enabled more and more to die unto sin, and live unto righteousness.*

(*a*) The phrase "to sanctify" is used in two different senses in Scripture—to consecrate, to set apart to a holy use (John 10 : 36; Matt. 23 : 17), and to render morally pure or holy (1 Cor. 6 : 11; Heb. 13 : 12). SANCTIFICATION is used in this latter sense. As REGENERATION is an *act* of God's free grace, so sanctification is a progressive work of the same free grace. It is gratuitous, for Christ's sake, and it is effected by the supernatural power of the Holy Ghost. (*b*) The *means* of sanctification are of two distinct orders—inward and outward.

The *inward* means of sanctification is Faith. Faith is the instrument of our justification, and hence of our deliverance from condemnation and of our communion with God; the organ of our union with Christ, and hence of our communion with him in his Spirit and life. Faith, moreover, is that act of the regenerated soul whereby it embraces and experiences the power of the truth, and whereby the inward experiences of the heart and the outward actions of the life are brought into obedience to the truth.

The *outward* means of sanctification are—

[1] The Truth as revealed in the inspired Scriptures (John 17 : 17, 19 ; 1 Pet. 1 : 22 ; 2 : 2).

[2] The Sacraments (Matt. 3 : 11 ; 1 Cor. 12 : 13 ; 1 Pet. 3 : 21).

[3] Prayer. This it effects both as a gracious exercise of the soul, and as the covenanted condition of our reception of all spiritual blessings (John 14 : 13, 14).

[4] The gracious discipline of God's providence (John 15 : 2 ; Rom. 5 : 3, 4 ; Heb. 12 : 5–11).

It must be remembered that the unregenerate soul resists the "common grace" with which the Holy Ghost wrestles with it previously to the new birth; also, that the soul is passive in respect to that particular exercise of the divine power which effects its regeneration or new birth. But having once been regenerated, the soul, now spiritually alive, continues to grow in grace by its own active co-operation with the gracious operations of the Holy Spirit, who dwells in it.

(*c*) The *fruits* of sanctification are—[1] Negatively, the destruction of the "old man," with its habits, affections, and lusts (Gal. 5 : 24 ; Col. 3 : 5). [2] Positively, the strengthening of the principle of grace, and the gradual training of all the faculties of the soul under the control of grace, in symmetrical development and holy obedience. [3] Hence, good works are the fruits of sanctification. These "good works," although never the meritorious grounds of acceptance before God, are nevertheless absolutely essential to salvation, because to be saved is to

SANCTIFICATION. 69

be saved *from* sin (Gal. 5 : 22, 23 ; Eph. 2 : 10; John 14 : 21).

(*d*) Sanctification involves the entire man, intellect, affections, and will (Eph. 1 ; 17, 18 ; Col. 3 : 10 ; 2 Cor. 4 : 6 ; 1 Thess. 5 : 23). Our bodies as integral parts of our persons are sanctified through their union with our spirits and the indwelling of the Holy Ghost (Rom. 6 : 13 ; 1 Cor. 6 :19 ; 1 Thess. 4 : 4).

(*e*) Perfect sanctification is never attained in this life. All Christian perfectionists admit that defects of knowledge, feeling, and will remain as long as we are in the body. But they claim that God has graciously, for Christ's sake, lowered the demands of the law, so that our present weaknesses, if only we do our best, are not accounted as sin.

This is a very dangerous heresy, because it lowers the moral standard of Christian character and the aim of Christian endeavor. The moral law of God under which Adam was created can never be lowered. All that is moral is essentially obligatory. All defect in love or active service is of the nature of sin. The best Christians are most humbly sensitive to their own defects, are daily filled with shame and contrition, and apply constantly to the cleansing blood of Christ and to the sanctifying power of the Holy Ghost.

The standard of Christian holiness is the holiness of God and the example of Christ.

Paul and John disclaim perfection (Rom 7 : 14–25 ; Phil. 3 : 12–14 ; 1 John 1 : 8). It is inconsistent with the experience of the best Christians and with the hymns and prayers of the historical churches.

The personal claim of sinless perfection is an evidence

of a low sense and standard of sin, of spiritual pride, and of a diseased self-consciousness. Experience shows that it is a very dangerous symptom, and presages a direful fall. The signs of grace are humility, eager desire to press on and advance to a higher standard, self-forgetfulness, absorption of thought and affection with Christ, entire consecration to the service of God and man.

(4) THE ACCOMPANYING BENEFITS. Ques. 36.

Q. 36. *What are the benefits which in this life do accompany or flow from justification, adoption, and sanctification.*

A. *The benefits which in this life do accompany or flow from justification, adoption, and sanctification, are, assurance of God's love, peace of conscience, joy in the Holy Ghost, increase of grace, and perseverance therein to the end.*

(*a*) ASSURANCE OF GOD'S LOVE. That act of saving faith whereby we embrace and appropriate Christ, which is the only instrument of our justification, involves *two* essential elements: [1] ASSENT is the intellectual recognition and cordial embrace of Christ and of his work; [2] TRUST is implicit reliance upon Christ alone for all our salvation (John 7 : 38; Acts 10 : 43; 16 : 31; 26 : 18; Gal. 2 : 16; 3 : 26; 2 Tim. 3 : 15). Trust rests upon the *foundation* upon which expectation is based. Hope reaches forward to the *object* upon which desire and expectation meet. Hope therefore rests upon that which trust rests upon, and trust gives birth and support to hope.

There is a difference, therefore, between the full *Assurance of Faith* (Heb. 10 : 22), which is strong, unwavering, unintermittent faith, and the full *Assurance of Hope* (Heb. 6 : 11), which is a result of the former, being a confident persuasion of our own personal salvation. "He that believes shall be saved :" this is made sure by the Word of God. "I believe :" this is a matter of consciousness and other evidence. "Therefore I am saved :" this is an infallible inference.

This conviction is not in such a sense of the essence of faith that every one who truly believes is consequently thus assured. Nevertheless, it is the privilege and duty of every believer to seek and to attain to this most comfortable and useful grace. "This certainty is not a bare conjectural and probable persuasion, grounded on a fallible hope, but an infallible assurance of faith (hope), founded upon the divine truth of the promises of salvation, the inward evidence of those graces unto which these promises are made, the testimony of the Spirit of Adoption witnessing with our spirits that we are the children of God; which Spirit is the earnest (pledge) of our inheritance, whereby we are sealed to the day of redemption" (Heb. 6 : 11, 19; Rom. 8 : 15, 16; Eph. 1 : 13, 14; 2 Pet. 1 : 4–11; 1 John 2 : 3; 3 : 14; 2 Cor. 1 : 12; CONFESSION OF FAITH, ch. 18).

This assurance may be dimmed and lost by inattention and yielding to sudden temptation, whereby our evidences are obscured and the Holy Spirit grieved. It may be revived or regained by sincere repentance, humble walking with God, the watchful avoidance of every approach to evil, and the diligent and prayerful use of all the means of grace.

(*b*) PEACE OF CONSCIENCE. Peace with God is reconciliation with him through the blood of Christ. Peace of conscience may either mean our consciousness of that reconciliation, or the appeasement by the same atoning blood of our own consciences, which otherwise condemn us. In the proportion in which our faith is clear and constant will be our consciousness of our reconciliation with God, and satisfaction of our own moral judgment that the law is maintained and righteousness is fulfilled, while yet we are saved from the penal consequences of our sin. If we diligently observe all God's commandments, "our peace shall be like a river" (Isa. 48 : 18). If it fail, it is our own fault.

(c) JOY IN THE HOLY GHOST. The Holy Ghost as the "Comforter" is the direct Author of joy in our hearts. Besides this, he is the indirect cause of joy to us, because, by uniting us to Christ and communicating to us his life and all the benefits of his redemption, he brings to us all the possible sources of joy. Besides, joy is an accompaniment of spiritual health. And this health is promoted by all the operations of the Holy Spirit in our hearts, and by the careful removal of all that grieves him and that hinders his work.

(d) INCREASE OF GRACE. The gifts of God are inexhaustible. We are not limited in him; we are only limited in ourselves. Each gift of grace leads to another. We are justified that we may be regenerated and sanctified. We are born babes in Christ that we may grow up to the stature of perfect manhood in him. If grace is improved, grace is added. The exercise of the lesser grace leads to an increase of capacity. With the increase of capacity will come the ever-proportionate increase of blessing, keeping the vessel ever full if we are faithful.

Then "dying grace" will succeed "living grace," and grace will be completed in glory.

(e) PERSEVERANCE IN GRACE TO THE END. The true believer, having once been regenerated and justified, will never be permitted finally to fall away and be lost. The doctrine is *not* that once a believer a man will be saved, do what he will; but it *is* that once a *true* believer God will ever uphold the man, so that he will freely persevere in faith and obedience to the end.

[1] The fact is proved from Scripture and experience (John 10:28; Rom. 11:29; Phil. 1:6; 1 Pet. 1:5).

[2] This *Perseverance of the Saints* in faith and holy obedience is not secured by their own purpose or strength, but by the immutable purpose of God and his covenant with his Son (John 10:29), and by the intercession of Christ (Luke 22:32), and by the constant indwelling and infinitely wise and constant care of the Holy Ghost (1 John 3:9; John 14:16, 17).

True believers may nevertheless fall into grievous sins, and for a time continue therein. The *occasions* of which falls are the temptations of the world, the seductions of Satan, the remaining corruptions of their own hearts, and the neglect of the means of grace. The *effects* of which falls are, that God is displeased and the Holy Spirit grieved; their comforts are lost, their minds darkened, their hearts hardened, and their consciences wounded, and often they are arrested by temporal judgments; their conduct is a stumbling-block to all witnesses and an occasion of sorrow to their fellow-Christians. Such experiences would be fatal if it were not for the faithfulness of God and the omnipotent power of his grace,

7th. THE BENEFITS CONFERRED BY THE APPLIED REDEMPTION OF CHRIST AT DEATH. Ques. 37.

Q. 37. *What benefits do believers receive from Christ at death?*

A. *The souls of believers are, at their death, made perfect in holiness, and do immediately pass into glory; and their bodies, being still united to Christ, do rest in their graves till the resurrection.*

(1) Death consists of the temporary dissolution of the personal union of soul and body. As long as this continues, the person is dead, and until the resurrection the soul, although holy and happy, as a disembodied spirit is under the power of death. Thus, our Larger Catechism says that "Christ continued in the state of the dead, and under the power of death, till the third day" (Ques. 50), when he ceased to be one of the dead, and became one of the living by rising from the dead.

(2) Immediately upon death "the souls of believers are made perfect in holiness." They should be growing in grace and holiness as long as they live. This process is consummated at death (*a*) by the power of the Holy Ghost, the divine Agent whereby the redemption purchased by Christ is applied in all its stages; (*b*) by the removal of the diseased and mortal body, and the consequent cessation of the "lust of the flesh" and the injurious struggle of "the law in our members" against " the law of our minds;" (*c*) and by the entire change of environment from this evil world and its spiritual conditions to heaven.

(3) At the same instant the soul of the believer passes into glory. The intermediate state is not final. The

THE STATE OF THE SOUL AFTER DEATH. 75

consummation of our salvation can come only after and in consequence of our resurrection. But in the mean time the holy soul, now made perfect, is in the presence of, and in the immediate fellowship with, Christ. Christ is already risen and glorified as "the first-fruits of them that sleep," and as such has sat down on the right hand of the Majesty on high. Paul's whole conception of heaven is expressed in the beautiful phrase, "To be present with the Lord" (2 Cor. 5 : 8). We know nothing as to the place of heaven, except that it is where Christ is now glorified in the presence of his saints. As to its happiness, we know that it will consist (*a*) in the total absence of sin and pain; (*b*) in the love of God and Christ; (*c*) in the vision of God in Christ; (*d*) in the perfect peace of God shed abroad in our hearts by the Holy Ghost, given now without measure; (*e*) in the blissful exercise of all our faculties in the service of God, and in the consequent ceaseless growth of all our powers; (*f*) in the blissful social relations of the redeemed and of the angelic hosts.

(4) "Their bodies being still united to Christ, do rest in their graves till the resurrection." The union established between the believer and Christ by faith includes his whole person, body as well as spirit. The body, although temporarily laid aside, is never alienated. It is always ours, and therefore it is always Christ's, for Christ has redeemed it by his blood and made it a temple of his Holy Ghost. "If we believe that Jesus died and rose again, even so them also which sleep in Jesus will God bring with him;" therefore, "our flesh also shall rest in hope" (1 Thess. 4 : 14; Ps. 16 : 9).

76 THE WESTMINSTER SYSTEM OF DOCTRINE.

8th. THE BENEFITS CONFERRED BY THE REDEMPTION OF CHRIST, THUS APPLIED, AT THE RESURRECTION. Ques. 38.

Q. 38. *What benefits do believers receive from Christ at the resurrection ?*

A. *At the resurrection, believers, being raised up in glory, shall be openly acknowledged and acquitted in the day of judgment, and made perfectly blessed in the full enjoying of God to all eternity.*

The time of the resurrection is not revealed. But the Scriptures teach that the following events are to occur together in immediate succession: (1) The Second Coming of Christ; (2) the Resurrection of the Evil and the Good; (3) the General Judgment; (4) the End of the World; (5) the Final Award of Rewards and Punishment (Matt. 24 : 30; Dan. 12 : 2; John 5 : 28, 29; 1 Cor. 15 : 23; 1 Thess. 4 : 16; Matt. 7 : 21, 23; 13 : 30–43; 16 : 24–27; 25 : 31–46; 2 Thess. 1 : 6–10; 2 Pet. 3 : 7–13).

This answer embraces *three* great subjects: (1) The Resurrection; (2) the Judgment; (3) Heaven.

(1) THE RESURRECTION.

(*a*) *All* men, good and bad, are to rise together, "they that have done good unto the resurrection of life, and they that have done evil unto the resurrection of damnation" (John 5 : 29). They who at that time are remaining alive on the earth will be changed and caught up to meet the coming Judge in the air (1 Thess. 4 : 17; 1 Cor. 15 : 51).

(*b*) The *same* bodies which are deposited in the graves shall be raised and united to their respective souls again (1 Cor. 15 : 42–44; 1 Thess. 4 : 14; John 5 : 28; 1 Thess. 4 : 13–17). The identical body of Christ rose

This identity does not depend upon sameness of material. From infancy to old age we have the selfsame bodies on earth, while their material constituents are continually changing. All we need to know is that our bodies in the resurrection will be in the same sense one with our bodies at death as our bodies at death are one with our bodies at birth.

(c) But they will be changed (not exchanged) in quality, and in all else necessary to adapt them [1] to the uses of our perfectly glorified souls in their high estate, and [2] to the physical conditions of the "new heavens and a new earth wherein dwelleth righteousness" (Rev. 21 : 1–5; 2 Pet. 3 : 13). They will be made like unto Christ's glorious body (Phil. 3 : 21). The present body is called "a natural body." The same body will become in heaven a "spiritual body." The word "spiritual" in the New Testament means that which is made a temple of the Holy Ghost, and is transformed by his indwelling (1 Cor. 2 : 12–15; 15 : 44).

(2) THE JUDGMENT.

(a) The Person who is to judge all men is the God-man, the same Person who was condemned at the bar of Pilate and executed as a malefactor on the cross. He will judge the world as Mediator (Matt. 25 : 31, 32; Acts 3 : 21; 17 : 31; John 5 : 22, 27; 2 Thess. 1 : 7–10; Rev. 1 : 7).

(b) The subjects of the judgment are to be all men who have ever lived and all fallen angels. The good angels will appear as attendants and ministers (Matt. 13 : 41, 42; 25 : 31–46; 1 Cor. 15 : 51, 52; 2 Cor. 5 : 10; 1 Thess. 4 : 17; 2 Thess. 1 : 6–10; Rev. 20 : 11–15; 2 Pet. 2 : 4; Jude 6).

(c) They will be judged [1] under the various degrees of light divinely revealed to each. "For as many as have sinned without law shall also perish without law. And as many as have sinned in the law, shall be judged by the law" (Rom. 2:12; Luke 12:47, 48). [2] The matter of the judgment will be all the deeds done in the body, including all "the secrets of the heart," "the deeds of darkness," the feelings, thoughts, purposes, and motives (Eccles. 12:14; 1 Cor. 4:5; Luke 8:17; 12:2,3; Matt. 12:36, 37). [3] The ground of justification and acquittal will be the righteousness of Christ and our personal relation to him, the work of Christ *for* us and the work of Christ *in* us (Phil. 4:3; Rev. 3:5; 13:8; 20:15; Matt. 13:43; 25:34–40).

(3) After the resurrection the salvation of believers will be complete. They will be *like* Christ, and *with* Christ for ever. What more can be said or thought? Their existence will every moment be perfect in excellence, usefulness, and blessedness, and for ever they will be advancing ceaselessly in knowledge, capacity, and in intimate fellowship with Christ, and hence in every possible good. "Eye hath not seen, nor ear heard, neither have entered into the heart of man, the things which God hath prepared for them that love him" (1 Cor. 2:9).

THE END OF PART I.

PART II.

DUTY REQUIRED OF MAN.

BY

REV. J ASPINWALL HODGE, D.D.

THE SYSTEM OF THEOLOGY

CONTAINED IN THE

WESTMINSTER SHORTER CATECHISM

EXHIBITED AND EXPLAINED.

PART II.

HAVING examined in Part I. what we are to believe concerning God, we are now to consider—

III. WHAT DUTY IS REQUIRED OF US.
Questions 39–81.

The consciousness of obligation is universal. Of even the heathen it is said, "They show the work of the law written in their hearts, their conscience also bearing witness" (Rom. 2 : 15). Any utterance of the will of God is recognized at once as obligatory, demanding immediate and perfect obedience (Deut. 5 : 1, 31, 33 ; Luke 10 : 26, 27 ; 1 Thess. 5 : 23).

The character of God's will, and therefore of our duty, depends upon what has already been considered—God's nature, his relations to us and purposes concerning us, as manifested in his works of creation, providence and redemption. If he be holy, "the law is holy and the commandment holy, just and good" (Rom. 7 : 12). If we be his creatures and his elect, formed, preserved and redeemed "to glorify God and enjoy him for ever," then we must be perfect as he is perfect, conformed unto his likeness (Gen. 1 : 26 ; 1 Pet. 1 : 16 ; Rom. 8 : 29). Therefore, this will of God is absolutely unchangeable, obligatory upon all and under all circumstances. It cannot be modified to suit man's ability. It was in force before and after the fall, and under both dispensations. It is the foundation of every covenant. Salvation is possible only by the perfect satisfaction of this law by Christ in behalf of his people, and we as such must keep his commandments (Romans).

We are to consider (1) our duty as revealed in the ten commandments; (2) the preface to them ; (3) the first table, as containing our duty to God ; and (4) the second table, our duty to man.

[I.] Our Duty as Revealed in the Ten Commandments. Ques. 39–42.

1st. OUR DUTY AS REVEALED.

Q. 39. *What is the duty which God requireth of man?*

A. *The duty which God requireth of man, is obedience to his revealed will.*

Q. 40. *What did God at first reveal to man for the rule of his obedience?*

A. *The rule which God at first revealed to man, for his obedience, was the moral law.*

It is the same law, however revealed—by God's works or word. In creation we perceive only " his eternal power and Godhead" (Rom. 1 : 20). His providence is often incomprehensible (Ps. 73). Therefore he has revealed his will in human language. The word of

THE MORAL LAW. 83

God is the only rule to direct us. It is a perfect rule. (1) It is the fullest and clearest revelation. (2) Its commands and prohibitions are final. (3) Nothing is sinful which it does not condemn, nor obligatory which it does not require.

This revealed law is called moral, because it concerns character, questions of right and wrong, holiness and sin. It is distinguished from (1) natural laws, as of day and night, bounds of the sea, growth and decay, etc. (Ps. 73 : 13–17 ; 104; Jer. 33 : 25) ; (2) the national law, that judicial code enjoined on the Jewish nation as such (Conf. of Faith, chap. xix. sect. iv.; Ex. 21 ; 22 : 1–29) ; (3) the ceremonial law, foretelling and prefiguring the redemption of Christ (Conf. of Faith, chap. xix. sec. iii.; Heb. 10 : 1 ; Gal. 4 : 1, 2, 3 ; Col. 2 : 14–17). These depending upon the present order of nature, the temporary condition of the Jews and the preparatory form of the mystery of salvation, all of which are transient, are temporary laws. But the moral law, based on the divine nature and on the fact that we were made in the image of God, is abiding and unchangeable.

This moral law was revealed to Adam in the manner and object of his creation, in his nature and in his constant communion with God (Gen. 1 : 26 ; 2 : 7 ; 3 : 8).

2d. THE SUMMARY OF OUR DUTY.

Q. 41. *Wherein is the moral law summarily comprehended?*

A. *The moral law is summarily comprehended in the ten commandments.*

Q. 42. *What is the sum of the ten commandments?*

A. *The sum of the ten commandments is, to love the Lord our God with all our heart, with all our soul, with*

84 THE WESTMINSTER SYSTEM OF DOCTRINE.

all our strength, and with all our mind; and our neighbor as ourselves.

At Sinai the covenant was renewed that God would be their God and they should be his people. What God required he expressed in the ten commandments, which he spake, and which he wrote on two tables of stone. Christ and the apostles refer to these as containing the duty of man (Ex. 20: 1–17; Deut. 5: 6–21; Mark 10 : 19; Rom. 13 : 9). The moral law is summarily comprehended in them. (1) They include our duty to God and to man; (2) all other directions for conduct are embraced in them; (3) they require perfect obedience through all time and from every part of our nature, mind, affections, will, as well as in word and deed.

The sum of the ten commandments is love—love to God, supreme love, with all our heart, with all our soul, with all our strength and with all our mind (Deut. 6 : 5; 10 : 12; Matt. 22 : 37); and love to man, our neighbor, as ourselves (Lev. 19 : 18; Matt. 5 : 43–48; 22 : 39; Rom. 13 : 9). Supreme love to God begets and includes love to man (1 John 3 : 14; 4 : 20).

Love is the sum of the commandments. (1) It is the highest form of, and therefore the only acceptable, obedience (John 21 : 15–17; 1 John 2 : 5). (2) The law requires likeness to God: God is love (1 John 4 : 8). (3) There is no obedience without love (Matt. 5 : 20; Deut. 10 : 12; Rom. 13 : 9). (4) Love must manifest itself in action and in the prescribed manner (**1 John 2 : 4**; 4 : 20; John 6 : 29; 14 : 15, 21, 23).

[II.] The Preface to the Ten Commandments. Ques. 43, 44.

Q. 43. *What is the preface to the ten commandments?*

A. *The preface to the ten commandments is in these words:* I AM THE LORD THY GOD, WHICH HAVE BROUGHT THEE OUT OF THE LAND OF EGYPT, OUT OF THE HOUSE OF BONDAGE.

Q. 44. *What doth the preface to the ten commandments teach us?*

A. *The preface to the ten commandments teacheth us, that because God is the Lord, and our God, and Redeemer, therefore we are bound to keep all his commandments.*

We have here stated the ground of obligation and the motives of obedience.

(1) The law comes from, not a principle, but a person who is in personal relation to those whom he commands: "I am."

(2) He is the Lord Jehovah, the self-existing, unchangeable and almighty Sovereign.

(3) He is God, Elohim, the only object of supreme worship, trust and obedience.

(4) He is our God, in peculiar relations to us, in covenant with us, not by our act or will, but because he chose us, first loved us, accepted us as his people and claimed a proprietorship in us, as he did in Israel because of his covenant with Abraham.

(5) He has already exercised his sovereignty and proprietorship in preserving and redeeming us. All providential care is the evidence and type of redemptive love. Deliverance from Egypt is frequently referred to as symbolizing freedom from the bondage of sin and Satan.

Therefore we are bound to keep all his commandments. It is to be noticed that in this preface and throughout the ten commandments the singular is used—"thy God," "brought thee out," "thou shalt"—indicating that the law was given, not merely to a nation nor to the multitude of the redeemed, but to each and every one personally, who must render a personal obedience.

The Larger Catechism gives us under Question 99 eight rules for the interpretation of the Decalogue, which may be thus expressed:

(1) The laws require the utmost perfection of every duty and forbid the least degree of every sin.

(2) They reach all the powers of the soul as well as all the actions of the body.

(3) The same thing in divers respects is required or forbidden in several commandments.

(4) Where a duty is enjoined the opposite sin is forbidden. A prohibition includes an order; a promise involves a threatening, and a threat a promise.

(5) These laws are always binding, yet every particular duty is not to be done at all times.

(6) Under one sin or duty all of the same kind are included, and everything that leads thereunto.

(7) These laws require us to see that they be observed by those under our control.

(8) We must help others in their obedience and have no part in their sins.

[III.] The First Table, as containing our Duty toward God. Ques. 45–62.

The law is divided into ten commandments. "He wrote, on the tables, the ten commandments" (Deut.

10 : 4), and these were written on two tables of stone (Deut. 4 : 13). The Jews called the preface the first law, and united the first and second and called it the second. The Latin and Lutheran churches joined the first and second and divided the tenth. Josephus, the Greek Church and the Reformed churches arranged them as in our English Bible and in this Catechism, because the preface is not in the form of a command, the first and second treat of different subjects, the clauses of the tenth refer to the one sin of covetousness, and each commandment begins with the same formula, except the fourth, which is evidently distinct.

These commandments are also divided into two tables, containing our duty to God and our duty to man. But some place five in each, regarding the fifth as requiring reverence to parents as representatives of God. Others, uniting the first and second and dividing the tenth, arrange three in the first and seven in the second table. The usual division, however, is that presented in our Catechism—four in the first, and six in the second—and the reasons are to be found in the nature of the commands.

I. THE FIRST COMMANDMENT: THE PERSON TO BE WORSHIPED. Ques. 45–48.

Q. 45. *Which is the first commandment?*

A. *The first commandment is*, THOU SHALT HAVE NO OTHER GODS BEFORE ME.

Q. 46. *What is required in the first commandment?*

A. *The first commandment requireth us to know and acknowledge God, to be the only true God, and our God; and to worship and glorify him accordingly.*

Q. 47. *What is forbidden in the first commandment?*

A. *The first commandment forbiddeth the denying, or not worshiping and glorifying the true God, as God, and our God; and the giving that worship and glory to any other, which is due to him alone.*

Q. 48. *What are we especially taught by these words, "* BEFORE ME*," in the first commandment?*

A. *These words, "* BEFORE ME*," in the first commandment, teach us, that God, who seeth all things, taketh notice of, and is much displeased with, the sin of having any other God.*

The first table includes the second. If we love God, we must love each other. And the first commandment necessitates and embraces all the rest. If we glorify God as our God, then we must render proper worship and must reverence his name and day.

The form of the questions emphasizes the fact that these prohibitions include the requirement of corresponding duties. Let us bear this in mind.

We are commanded—

(1) To have but one only object of supreme love, obedience and worship. There is, in fact, but one God (Deut. 6 : 4 ; Isa. 43 : 10 ; Jer. 10 : 10 ; 14 : 22 ; 1 Cor. 8 : 4, 6).

(2) To know this one God as he has revealed himself, as the God of nature, the God in covenant, and especially in his latest and clearest manifestation in Christ Jesus, the Saviour and final Judge. (See the preface ; Matt. 11 : 27 ; John 1 : 14 ; 1 Tim. 3 : 16 ; Heb. 1 : 3.)

(3) To acknowledge him as our God by open confession and in acts of obedience and worship (Deut. 26 : 17 ; John 10 : 27 ; Rom. 10 : 9, 10).

(4) To worship him in adoration, prayer and service (Isa. 45 : 23; Rom. 12 : 11).

We are forbidden—

(1) To neglect, delay or qualify these duties.

(2) To take part in the worship of any false god (Hos. 4 : 12; Rom. 1 : 25).

(3) To invoke angels, saints, Mary, the pope or priests as objects of worship or as intercessors with God (Col. 2 : 18; Rev. 19 : 10).

(4) To consult directly or indirectly the spirits of men or of devils, or to seek from them the knowledge which belongs only to God (Lev. 20 : 6; 1 Sam. 28 : 7–20; 1 Cor. 10 : 20; Rev. 9 : 20).

All this is enforced by the fact that disobedience is a personal insult to God and in his presence ("before me"), and that he will punish it.

II. THE SECOND COMMANDMENT: THE FORM OF WORSHIP. Ques. 49–52.

Q. 49. *Which is the second commandment?*

A. *The second commandment is,* THOU SHALT NOT MAKE UNTO THEE ANY GRAVEN IMAGE, OR ANY LIKENESS OF ANY THING THAT IS IN HEAVEN ABOVE, OR THAT IS IN THE EARTH BENEATH, OR THAT IS IN THE WATER UNDER THE EARTH; THOU SHALT NOT BOW DOWN THYSELF TO THEM, NOR SERVE THEM; FOR I THE LORD THY GOD AM A JEALOUS GOD, VISITING THE INIQUITY OF THE FATHERS UPON THE CHILDREN, UNTO THE THIRD AND FOURTH GENERATION OF THEM THAT HATE ME, AND SHOWING MERCY UNTO THOUSANDS OF THEM THAT LOVE ME AND KEEP MY COMMANDMENTS.

Q. 50. *What is required in the second commandment?*

A. *The second commandment requireth the receiving, observing, and keeping pure and entire, all such religious worship and ordinances, as God hath appointed in his word.*

Q. 51. *What is forbidden in the second commandment?*

A. *The second commandment forbiddeth the worshiping of God by images, or any other way not appointed in his word.*

Q. 52. *What are the reasons annexed to the second commandment?*

A. *The reasons annexed to the second commandment are, God's sovereignty over us, his propriety in us, and the zeal he hath to his own worship.*

This commandment prescribes the manner or form of worship. It requires—

(1) That it be spiritual. "God is a Spirit, and they that worship him must worship him in spirit and in truth" (John 4 : 24; Deut. 4 : 15–18).

(2) And external, for we are in the flesh and in a material world (Joel 2 : 12, 13; 1 Cor. 14 : 23–40).

(3) The outward acts must be expressive of feelings, and especially of faith (Isa. 29 : 13; Matt. 15 : 8; Heb. 11).

(4) God has prescribed the form of worship. It must always consist of praise, prayer and instruction. Under the Old Testament dispensation public worship was ceremonial, sacrificial and spectacular, but always typical of Christ and expressive of faith in him (Gen. 4 : 4, 5; see ceremonial law). In the New Testament it is very simple, free and under the direction of the Spirit, and to this we are required to adhere. (See Acts; Col. 2 : 13–23.)

It forbids—

(1) The worship of false gods, and everything that represents them (Acts 17 : 29 ; Rom. 1 : 21–25).

(2) The worship of God by images. Pictures and other representations of created things are allowed us in works of art or for ornamentation. God ordered the making of the serpent of brass and the figures in the temple. But they are not to be used in worship (Deut. 4 : 15–19 ; Ex. 32 : 5 ; Num. 21 : 9 ; 2 Kings 18 : 4). This was the sin of Israel until the Babylonish captivity. Pictures and images were first introduced into the Christian Church for instruction, then as helps in worship, and finally as objects of reverence.

(3) A ceremonial or ritual service, after the more spiritual form, has been enjoined (Acts 15 : 10–29 ; Rom. 14 : 17 ; Gal. 2 : 11–14 ; 3 : 3 ; 4 : 1–11).

(4) The neglect of God's ordinances, public worship and the sacraments (Heb. 10 : 25 ; Acts 2 : 42 ; Matt. 26 : 26, 27 ; John 6 : 53).

This commandment is enforced by—

(1) God's authority over us.

(2) His right to determine how he shall be worshiped.

(3) A curse to the third and fourth generations.

(4) A blessing which is unending in duration and extent.

III. THE THIRD COMMANDMENT: THE SPIRIT OF WORSHIP. Ques. 53–56.

Q. 53. *Which is the third commandment?*

A. *The third commandment is,* THOU SHALT NOT TAKE THE NAME OF THE LORD THY GOD IN VAIN:

FOR THE LORD WILL NOT HOLD HIM GUILTLESS THAT TAKETH HIS NAME IN VAIN.

Q. 54. *What is required in the third commandment?*

A. *The third commandment requireth the holy and reverent use of God's names, titles, attributes, ordinances, word and works.*

Q. 55. *What is forbidden in the third commandment?*

A. *The third commandment forbiddeth all profaning or abusing of anything whereby God maketh himself known.*

Q. 56. *What is the reason annexed to the third commandment?*

A. *The reason annexed to the third commandment is, that however the breakers of this commandment may escape punishment from men, yet the Lord our God will not suffer them to escape his righteous judgment.*

We are to worship God with reverence (Deut. 6 : 13; 28 : 58)

In Scripture, "*name*" expresses nature and character and that by which these are manifested. The name of God includes, therefore, his titles, attributes, ordinances, word and works. "*In vain*" means either irreverently, as in profanity, or falsely, as in perjury. The meaning is the same, for perjury includes all that leads to it—deception, lying and irreverence toward the God of truth.

We are required to treat with great reverence everything whereby God maketh himself known.

An oath is an act of worship, wherein we invoke God, as God knowing all things and as final Judge, to hear our declaration and to approve or punish. It may be in assertion, as in witness-bearing, or in promise, as in oath of office. Oaths are lawful—(1) being acts of worship; (2) often commanded by God (Ex. 22 : 11); (3) Christ used them (Heb. 6 : 13; Matt. 26 : 63). They may be required by authority (Matt. 26 : 63) or offered between man and man (Gen. 24 : 3; 47 : 31; 2 Cor. 1 : 23). Christ (in Matt. 5 : 33–37) forbids irreverent and unnecessary or trivial appeals to God, and all profane swearing.

A vow is also an act of worship, wherein we consecrate something to God and his service.

Oaths and vows are not binding when the performance of them would be contrary to God's revealed will. The sin is in the making, not in the keeping of such (Acts 23 : 12, 14; Mark 6 : 26; 1 Sam. 25 : 22, 32).

We are forbidden—

(1) All deception, falsehood and perjury.

(2) All irreverence of God's name, as in the careless use of his names, attributes and ordinances for emphasis in conversation or expressions of surprise, as well as in profane swearing; and the use of God's word in jesting, in tempting or in upholding false doctrine (Jer. 23 : 34–38; Matt. 4 : 6; 27 : 47; 2 Pet. 3 : 16).

All this is enforced by the determination of God to punish those who treat him or his cause with disrespect.

IV. THE FOURTH COMMANDMENT: THE TIME FOR WORSHIP. Ques. 57–62.

Q. 57. *Which is the fourth commandment?*

A. *The fourth commandment is*, REMEMBER THE SABBATH DAY TO KEEP IT HOLY. SIX DAYS SHALT THOU LABOR, AND DO ALL THY WORK: BUT THE SEVENTH DAY IS THE SABBATH OF THE LORD THY GOD: IN IT THOU SHALT NOT DO ANY WORK, THOU,

NOR THY SON, NOR THY DAUGHTER, THY MAN-SERVANT, NOR THY MAID-SERVANT, NOR THY CATTLE, NOR THY STRANGER THAT IS WITHIN THY GATES; FOR IN SIX DAYS THE LORD MADE HEAVEN AND EARTH, THE SEA, AND ALL THAT IN THEM IS, AND RESTED THE SEVENTH DAY: WHEREFORE THE LORD BLESSED THE SABBATH DAY AND HALLOWED IT.

Q. 58. *What is required in the fourth commandment?*

A. *The fourth commandment requireth the keeping holy to God, such set times as he hath appointed in his word; expressly one whole day in seven, to be a holy Sabbath to himself.*

Q. 59. *Which day of the seven hath God appointed to be the weekly Sabbath?*

A. *From the beginning of the world to the resurrection of Christ, God appointed the seventh day of the week to be the weekly Sabbath; and the first day of the week, ever since, to continue to the end of the world, which is the Christian Sabbath.*

Q. 60. *How is the Sabbath to be sanctified?*

A. *The Sabbath is to be sanctified by a holy resting all that day, even from such worldly employments and recreations as are lawful on other days; and spending the whole time in the public and private exercises of God's worship, except so much as is to be taken up in the works of necessity and mercy.*

Q. 61. *What is forbidden in the fourth commandment?*

A. *The fourth commandment forbiddeth the omission, or careless performance, of the duties required, and the profaning the day by idleness, or doing that which is in itself sinful or by unnecessary thoughts, words, or works, about our worldly employments or recreations.*

THE FOURTH COMMANDMENT. 95

Q. 62. *What are the reasons annexed to the fourth commandment?*

A. *The reasons annexed to the fourth commandment are, God's allowing us six days of the week for our own employments, his challenging a special propriety in the seventh, his own example, and his blessing the Sabbath day.*

The time required for worship, especially public and united, is one full day in seven. And this is to be rendered as an acknowledgment that all time belongs to God, and that every day we are bound to glorify him. The appointment of a set day for public worship includes the duty of having regular and frequent times for secret, family and social prayer (Ezek. 20 : 12, 19, 20 ; Matt. 6 : 6 ; Job 1 : 6 ; Ps. 119 : 164).

The object is (1) to secure rest from worldly labor and pleasures. This is important, but is too often regarded as its principal aim. It is only preparatory to the chief object, (2) to secure a full day of uninterrupted worship of God, an important part of which is instruction. This is evident from (*a*) the place of this law in the Decalogue; (*b*) the use of the terms "to keep it holy," "sanctified it," "blessed it," "hallowed it," "the Sabbath of the Lord thy God;" (*c*) its design, to commemorate the creation, the deliverance from Egypt (Deut. 5 : 15), and therefore the redemption by Christ.

This law is still obligatory, because—

(1) It is one of the ten commandments.

(2) It is necessary from man's nature as a moral and immortal being, pressed by the labors and enticements of this fleeting world.

(3) It is in fact perpetual. It has been observed from

the creation, under the patriarchal, Mosaic and Christian dispensations, and will be to the end of time.

(4) God's blessing follows its observance (Isa. 56 : 2, 4, 6, 7).

It must be sanctified according to—

(1) The definite directions here given.

(2) Its design, as an entire day of united public worship, by all in the house, under our authority and influence and within the gates of the city.

(3) The example of Christ and his apostles. He removed the traditions of the Pharisees, but obeyed this divine law, attending synagogue and temple services, preaching and doing deeds of mercy (Luke 4 : 16; 6 : 1–11; 13 : 11–17; Matt. 12 : 1–13). So did his disciples.

The day to be observed is important. Under the old dispensation it was the seventh day of the week, commemorative of the creation, and God's sovereignty over all. Under the new dispensation it is the first day, setting forth the new creation, and God's redemption offered to all. The change was made for a sufficient reason, as just indicated, and by divine authority.

(1) Christ rose from the dead and appeared to his disciples frequently on the first day of the week (Matt. 28 : 1–10; John 20 :).

(2) It is called the Lord's Day (Rev. 1 : 10).

(3) The inspired apostles recognized and encouraged its observance in the Christian Church (Acts 20 : 7; 1 Cor. 16 : 1, 2; Rev. 1 : 10).

(4) It has been, and is, the weekly Sabbath of the Christian world, and it receives God's approbation.

(5) It is used as a type of heaven (Heb. 4 : 4–11).

This law forbids—

(1) All unnecessary work on the Sabbath by ourselves, by those under our control or influence and by our cattle. The only exceptions which Christ made were works of necessity and mercy, as the care of living creatures, the relief of the suffering and necessary labor in maintaining public worship (Matt. 12 : 1–13).

(2) The substitution of bodily rest or of social amusement for the worship of God, which is the real object of the Sabbath. (See Conf. of Faith, chap. xxi., and Larger Catechism, Ques. 116–119.)

(3) The careless, formal or irregular worship of God.

The reasons annexed to this law are more numerous than to any other commandment: (1) His gift to us of six other days; (2) his claim of special proprietorship in the Sabbath; (3) his example; (4) his benediction and implied curse.

[IV.] The Second Table, as containing our Duty toward Men. Ques. 63–81.

We have already noticed how intimately this table is connected with the first. The fifth commandment is a fit connecting-link, possessing many of the characteristics of both, and it embraces all the commandments that follow, for if we rightly observe our relations to men, we will maintain each other's rights in all things.

The sum of this table is "to love our neighbor as ourselves."

It contains six commandments, which concern (I.) our mutual relations, and (II.) our involved rights to life, purity, property, truth and contentment.

I. THE FIFTH COMMANDMENT: OUR MUTUAL RELATIONS. Ques. 63–66.

Q. 63. *Which is the fifth commandment?*

A. *The fifth commandment is,* HONOR THY FATHER AND THY MOTHER: THAT THY DAYS MAY BE LONG UPON THE LAND WHICH THE LORD THY GOD GIVETH THEE.

Q. 64. *What is required in the fifth commandment?*

A. *The fifth commandment requireth the preserving the honor of, and performing the duties, belonging to every one in their several places and relations, as superiors, inferiors, or equals.*

Q. 65. *What is forbidden in the fifth commandment?*

A. *The fifth commandment forbiddeth the neglecting of, or doing anything against, the honor and duty which belongeth to every one in their several places and relations.*

Q. 66. *What is the reason annexed to the fifth commandment?*

A. *The reason annexed to the fifth commandment is, a promise of long life and prosperity (as far as it shall serve for God's glory, and their own good) to all such as keep this commandment.*

Our relations to each other as superiors, inferiors or equals have been ordained by God, and he has determined their character and the duties involved in them. Their design is—(1) To reveal his relations to us. He is our Father, Brother, King, Master, etc. (Mal. 1 : 6; Matt. 6 : 9; John 18 : 37). (2) To maintain order, mutual responsibilities and co-operation and good feeling among men (Rom. 12 : 10; 1 Pet. 2 : 13, 14). (3) To prepare us for closer associations in his house above (Eph. 2 : 19–22). As we therefore enter into these relations, we are brought under new obligations to God,

THE FIFTH COMMANDMENT. 99

and the fidelity required is to God more than to each other (Eph 5 : 21–6 : 9).

The filial relation is specified, because—

(1) It is the first into which we enter, and ordinarily it continues longer than any other. At birth we are sons, and we continue under parental authority as long as father and mother are spared to us, and in time we become parents ourselves. The Scriptures nowhere recognize freedom from filial duty because of age or the forming of other ties (Gen. 43 : 1–14; John 19 : 26, 27).

(2) It includes all others: the family becomes the state and the church when modified and enlarged. (See Old and New Testament history.)

(3) It is the most perfect type of our relation to God, most absolute, loving and abiding. At first entire submission is required, and as we are developed in our faculties we render more intelligent and loving obedience.

These relations are either (1) personal, as fraternal, friendly, between husband and wife, or employer and employee. Some of these are natural, and others are voluntary. The latter involve an additional responsibility as to the persons with whom we enter them, and as to the time of beginning and ending them; in all which we should be directed by the word of God (Ps. 1 : 1; 2 Cor. 6 : 14; Matt. 5 : 31, 32). (2) Social, as in societies, especially in the State and the Church. These also are God's ordinances, and should be framed according to his revealed will (Rom. 13 : 1–6; Heb. 13 : 17; Matt. 18 : 17). When imperfect, or contrary to the divine plan in form or laws, they are to be respected and obeyed while in force, so far as we conscientiously can, and their penalties endured when we for Christ's sake must disobey (Acts 4 : 19 ; Heb. 11 : 32–39; 1 Pet. 2 : 19, 20).

The requirements and prohibitions are determined by the nature of each relation as revealed by God, and not as interpreted by human laws, traditions or customs, or by personal opinions. The honor required is respect and love manifested in word and deed, modified in each case by the nature of the several relations. Christ (in Mark 7 : 9–13 and elsewhere) removed the pharisaical interpretations and reinforced this commandment (Luke 2 : 51). So did the apostles.

The promise annexed has special reference to the filial relation (Eph. 6 : 1–3), but the blessing of long life and prosperity belongs also to those who are faithful in other relations (Ps. 91 : 16 ; Prov. 3 : 2 ; Col. 3 : 24).

II. OUR MUTUAL RIGHTS, AS INVOLVED IN THESE RELATIONS. Ques. 67–81.

1st. THE SIXTH COMMANDMENT. OUR RIGHT TO LIFE. Ques. 67–69.

Q. 67. *Which is the sixth commandment?*

A. *The sixth commandment is,* THOU SHALT NOT KILL.

Q. 68. *What is required in the sixth commandment?*

A. *The sixth commandment requireth all lawful endeavors to preserve our own life, and the life of others.*

Q. 69. *What is forbidden in the sixth commandment?*

A. *The sixth commandment forbiddeth the taking away of our own life, or the life of our neighbor unjustly, or whatsoever tendeth thereunto.*

We have a right to the life—

(1) Of the body, as given and preserved by God, for his glory, our good and the welfare of others.

THE SIXTH COMMANDMENT. 101

(2) Of the soul, as purchased by Christ and offered as a free gift to us, and through us to others.

These are closely connected, for eternal life is proffered to us and by us to our fellows, only while we are in the flesh. Death ends probation (Luke 16 : 22–31).

We are required to preserve our own life and that of others, because—

1. Of the importance of life, as above stated (Matt. 16 : 26).

2. We were made in the likeness of God (Gen. 1 : 27 ; 9 : 6).

3. It is God's prerogative to give and take away life (Gen. 30 : 2 ; Deut. 32 : 39).

4. Life is the appointed time for the service of God (John 9 : 4).

We are to preserve it by—

(1) Attention to the known laws of health as to food, shelter, exercise, rest and remedies, by which our whole nature is developed, kept in full vigor or restored when injured or impaired (Luke 21 : 34 ; Rom. 13 : 13 ; Col. 2 : 23).

(2) Holy living (Col. 3 : 12–14, 23–25).

(3) Calm dependence upon God in duties, temptations and trials (Matt. 6 : 34 ; 1 Pet. 5 : 7 ; Heb. 12 : 5–13).

(4) Peaceable and loving conduct toward men (1 Cor. 13 : 4, 5 ; Rom. 13 : 10 ; Prov. 10 : 12 ; Eph. 4 : 31).

(5) Defence of self and others, without malice, restraining and opposing the violence of others. When really necessary this defence may be even unto death (Ex. 22 : 2).

What is true of individuals is true of communities, and therefore under some circumstances war is justifiable. It is so recognized in the Old and New Testaments. (See Deut. 22; Rom. 13 : 4; Heb. 11 : 32–34.)

The sins forbidden are—

(1) "The neglecting or withdrawing the lawful or necessary means of preservation of life; sinful anger, hatred, envy, desire of revenge; all excessive passions, distracting cares; immoderate use of meat, drink, labor and recreations; provoking words; oppression, quarreling, striking, wounding, and whatsoever else tends to the destruction of the life of any" (Larger Catechism, Q. 136).

(2) The engaging in any occupation, habit or amusement which jeopardizes or shortens life (Matt. 4 : 6, 7 ; Luke 21 : 34; Phil. 3 : 18, 19; Ps. 55 : 23; Prov. 23 : 29–35; 2 Sam. 23 : 17).

(3) The refusing known remedies when sick (1 Tim. 5 : 23), and the use of unnecessary or improper drugs.

(4) Dueling, which, so far from being justifiable, is (a) in intention a deliberate double murder by each party, (b) without cause—the laws of God and man supply a sufficient remedy; (c) no solution of the difficulty, but is merely a trial of nerve and skill.

(5) Child-murder, whether before or after birth, by direct or indirect means (Ex. 21 : 22, 23; Acts 7 : 19).

(6) Suicide, as (a) assuming God's prerogative, (b) deserting appointed work, (c) demanding judgment before the time, (d) bringing shame, sorrow and loss upon others.

(7) Lynch law. Capital punishment is enjoined in Scripture for several offences under the Jewish code and the ceremonial law, which, as we have seen, are no longer obligatory. As the penalty for murder, it belongs to the moral law, (a) enforced before the Flood (Gen. 4 : 14, 24), (b) reiterated to Noah, the second head of

the race (Gen. 9 : 4-6), (c) necessitated by man's relation to man (Ex. 21 : 14), (d) and by his relation to God (Num. 35 : 30, 31), (e) recognized in the New Testament (Acts 25 : 11 ; Heb. 10 : 28). But in all cases it must be inflicted by legal authority and after formal trial (Rom. 13 : 4).

Christ shows (in Matt. 5 : 38-48) that this commandment extends to thoughts, words and feelings, as well as to deeds of violence, and he demands love to enemies and persecutors. (See his promised blessing in Matt. 5 : 9-12.)

2d. THE SEVENTH COMMANDMENT. OUR RIGHT TO PURITY. Ques. 70-72.

Q. 70. *Which is the seventh commandment?*

A. *The seventh commandment is,* THOU SHALT NOT COMMIT ADULTERY.

Q. 71. *What is required in the seventh commandment?*

A. *The seventh commandment requireth the preservation of our own and our neighbor's chastity, in heart, speech, and behavior.*

Q. 72. *What is forbidden in the seventh commandment?*

A. *The seventh commandment forbiddeth all unchaste thoughts, words, and actions.*

We have the right to personal purity, and are bound to secure it to each other. We were created in the image of God, "to glorify him in our bodies and spirits, which are his." By redemption Christ reasserts his claims to our persons. He makes his abode within us; our bodies become "the temples of the Holy Ghost," the abode of God, the place and instrument for his worship and service. Any impurity defiles the temple of God (1 Cor. 3 : 16, 17 ; 6 : 13, 19 ; 2 Cor. 6 : 16),

104 THE WESTMINSTER SYSTEM OF DOCTRINE.

Adultery is a very heinous sin—(1) for the above reason (1 Cor. 6 : 18); (2) it involves the breaking of solemn covenants (Mal. 2 : 14, 15); (3) unlike other sins, it requires a participator, whose guilt must also be shared.

In Matt. 5 : 27, 28, Christ declares that this commandment extends to thoughts and looks as well as to words and deeds of uncleanness (Matt. 15 : 19). He and his apostles make frequent reference to this sin, and urge upon us constant watchfulness, the keeping our bodies under control, the avoidance of places, persons and objects of temptation, the cultivation of chaste conversation and conduct, the preserving the purity of others and diligence in holy work and influence.

The requirements and prohibitions are more fully expressed in the Larger Catechism, which will repay careful study. In this list of things forbidden we find "idleness, gluttony, drunkenness, unchaste company; lascivious songs, books, pictures, dancing, stage-plays, and all other provocations to, or acts of, uncleanness, either in ourselves or others" (Ques. 139).

This subject requires us to consider—

(1) *Celibacy*, which is not a more virtuous, but a lower, state than matrimony.

(*a*) God made man male and female (Gen. 1 : 27, 28 ; Matt. 19 : 4).

(*b*) Marriage is declared to be the normal state, the best in which to do God's work (Gen. 2 : 18, 23–25; 1 Cor. 7 : 2 ; 1 Tim. 5 : 14).

(*c*) Celibacy was regarded as a calamity and a reproach (Jud. 11 : 37 ; Ps. 78 : 63 ; Isa. 4 : 1).

(*d*) In the New Testament marriage is said to be

THE SEVENTH COMMANDMENT. 105

honorable in all, and is enjoined (Matt. 19 : 5; Eph. 5 : 31; 1 Cor. 7 : 2; 1 Tim. 5 : 14; Heb. 13 : 4).

(e) "Forbidding to marry" is part of the "doctrine of devils" (1 Tim. 4 : 3).

(f) Marriage is the symbol of our union to Christ (Isa. 54 : 5; 62 : 5; Eph. 5 : 22–33; Rev. 21 : 9).

(g) Celibacy is recommended only in times of trouble or in emergencies in Christian work (1 Cor. 7 : 6–9, 25–40; Matt. 19 : 10–12; 24 : 19).

(2) *Polygamy.* A few cases are recorded—one in Cain's seed (Gen. 4 : 23), and others among the patriarchs and kings and princes in the later history. But it appears (a) to have been confined to persons in high official positions, and in imitation of heathen practices or from improper motives; (b) to be unrecognized and unapproved by the law; (c) as receiving divine providential reproof (see the history of each case); and (d) condemned in the New Testament (Matt. 19 : 5; 1 Cor. 7 ; 2).

(3) *Prohibited Marriages.* It is generally admitted that the Mosaic laws in this respect are still binding, except a few regulations which evidently belong to the ceremonial and judicial codes. They are in force, because—

(a) These laws concern human relations as such.

(b) Of the reason given in each case, nearness of kin, which is neither typical nor Jewish.

(c) If not in force, there is no Bible injunction against any form of incest.

These prohibitions regard husband and wife as one, and therefore the kin of one is kin of the other (Lev. 18 : 16; 20 : 21; Matt. 14 : 4).

The New Testament interprets and enforces the Levitical law, and requires that we marry "only in the Lord" (1 Cor. 7 : 39; 2 Cor. 6 : 14; Ex. 34 : 16).

(4) *Divorce.* It is admitted that (*a*) under the old dispensation divorces were in certain cases permitted (because of "uncleanness," Deut. 24 : 1); (*b*) that tradition and custom greatly increased this license; and (*c*) that Christ restored the marriage law to its original standing (Matt. 19 : 3–9). The only question is, What are the scriptural grounds for divorce? Marriage is a divine institution, and the state cannot determine when it shall be annulled.

(*a*) Adultery is a just ground (Matt. 5 : 32; 19 : 9).

(*b*) Willful desertion by an unbeliever (infidel or heathen) because of the Christian faith of the partner (1 Cor. 7 : 12–17). Many authorities, as indeed our Confession of Faith (chap. xxiv. sec. vi.), draw from this the inference that any persistent willful desertion is a just cause for divorce, yet the terms of the text seem very explicit.

(*c*) No other ground is recognized in Scripture.

3d. THE EIGHTH COMMANDMENT. OUR RIGHT TO PROPERTY. Ques. 73–75.

Q. 73. *Which is the eighth commandment?*

A. *The eighth commandment is,* THOU SHALT NOT STEAL.

Q. 74. *What is required in the eighth commandment?*

A. *The eighth commandment requireth the lawful procuring and furthering the wealth and outward estate of ourselves and others.*

Q. 75. *What is forbidden in the eighth commandment?*

A. *The eighth commandment forbiddeth whatsoever*

THE EIGHTH COMMANDMENT.

doth, or may, unjustly hinder our own, or our neighbor's wealth or outward estate.

We have a right to property, and are bound to respect that of others.

This right of exclusive possession and use is not from mutual consent nor civil law, but from God.

(1) The earth was given to man, and he is to have dominion over all it contains (Gen. 1 : 26–28; Ps. 115 : 16).

(2) To Adam God gave the garden and its fruits (Gen. 2 : 8–17); to nations, the bounds of their habitations (Acts 17 : 26); to Israel, to each tribe, household and person, a possession (Gen. 13 : 14–18; Josh. 14 : –21 :).

(3) Throughout Scripture, God is said to give or withhold worldly goods (Gen. 31 : 16; 1 Sam. 2 : 7; Matt. 6 : 32; Luke 1 : 53).

(4) He demanded tithes as an acknowledgment that all belonged to him (Lev. 27 : 30–34).

(5) He determines how, and for what, property shall be used. (See below.)

(6) And he will require an account (Matt. 25 : 19–46).

(7) Even heaven is an inheritance (Eph. 1 : 11–18; Col. 1 : 12).

Civil law must recognize this right, secure it, and determine the means and terms by which property is to be held, defended, conveyed and transmitted.

It may be rightly acquired by inheritance, gift, purchase, mental or physical labor, use and usury. When usury is condemned in Scripture undue rates and disregard to the condition of the borrower are meant (Ez. 18 : 8; 22 : 12; Ps. 15 : 5). The specified use is God's glory, in the maintenance of our households (1 Tim. 5 : 8), in helping the poor and needy (Matt. 25 : 31–46; Acts 2 : 45; 1 Cor. 16 : 1), and in advancing Christ's Church (Rom. 10 : 15; 1 Cor. 9 : 11; Rev. 21 : 24).

Personal and exclusive right to own, use and dispose of one's possessions has always been recognized. Yet property may be held under different systems.

(1) In the times of the patriarchs, the land outside of cities and villages seems to have been regarded as free to the use of all, while wells, burying-places and land temporarily used for growing crops were, with flocks, herds, tents, etc., personal possessions.

(2) Under the theocracy the whole land was divided to families as their permanent inheritance, which, if sold, would be restored in the year of jubilee.

(3) In Jerusalem after Pentecost community of goods was established. But we should notice—(*a*) Though allowed, it was not recommended nor indorsed by the apostles. (*b*) It was adopted only in that city and for a little while in the Christian Church. (*c*) It was not enforced nor general even there. (*d*) The personal right to property before and after sale, and to the whole or part of the price, was distinctly recognized (Acts 2 : 44, 45; 4 : 32–5 : 11). (*e*) It is maintained by many that "they had all things common" is explained by the preceding clause, "neither said any of them that aught of the things which he possessed was his own" (Acts 4 : 32). (*f*) Whenever attempted in later years it has failed of good results.

(4) Communism and Socialism have often been tried. Although different, they are closely connected and are

seldom found separated, even in theory. The system includes a denial of God and of his authority in our relations and rights, and a denial of individual possession of real estate, of personal property, of the rewards of labor and skill. All things are held for the common good, and distribution is made according to the needs of each irrespective of diligence. This leads to real Socialism, the holding that relationships also are for the use of all, and are to be continued only according to mutual consent. This is atheistical and revolutionary, and is destructive in proportion to its success.

(5) The system now generally adopted is that which recognizes the individual and exclusive right to acquire by lawful means, and to enjoy, use, increase, dispose of and transmit, both real and personal property. In the exercise of this right we are to be regulated by our accountability to God and by our mutual relations to each other, by love to God and love to man. We are therefore required to use all lawful means for "the procuring and furthering the wealth and outward estate of ourselves and others."

We are forbidden to unjustly hinder the wealth of ourselves or others. This is often done by theft, tricks of trade, misrepresentations, adulterations, breach of trust, bribery, withholding wages, oppression, strikes, interference with the labor or business of others, taking advantage of ignorance or necessity or of technicalities in law, by idleness or wastefulness, by gambling (which includes all forms of obtaining goods by chance without a just equivalent), by penuriousness, by the lack of benevolence and brotherly love, etc. etc. (See Larger Catechism, Ques. 141, 142.)

4th. THE NINTH COMMANDMENT. OUR RIGHT TO TRUTH. Ques. 76–78.

Q. 76. *Which is the ninth commandment?*

A. *The ninth commandment is,* THOU SHALT NOT BEAR FALSE WITNESS AGAINST THY NEIGHBOR.

Q. 77. *What is required in the ninth commandment?*

A. *The ninth commandment requireth the maintaining and promoting of truth between man and man, and of our own and our neighbor's good name, especially in witness-bearing.*

Q. 78. *What is forbidden in the ninth commandment?*

A. *The ninth commandment forbiddeth whatsoever is prejudicial to truth, or injurious to our own, or our neighbor's good name.*

We have a right to truth concerning and toward ourselves and others.

(1) Truth is one of the essential characteristics of God, to whose likeness we must be conformed (Ps. 31 : 5 ; 57 : 10 ; John 14 : 6 ; Rom. 3 : 4).

(2) God gives and demands it (Ps. 12 ; 51 : 6 ; Eph. 4 : 15, 25).

(3) Our security under God's government depends on the truth of its principles and the certainty of its execution (Ps. 89 : 34 ; Jer. 33 : 20 ; Ex. 20 : 5).

(4) Truth is essential in all our dealings with men (Jer. 20 : 10 ; Prov. 29 : 2 ; Rom. 1 : 29–32).

Therefore a liar is a rebel against God and must be excluded from heaven (Rev. 21 : 8), and an enemy of mankind and unfit to associate with men (Deut. 33 : 29). The term "liar" is regarded by all as the most fearful accusation and insult.

We are required to—

THE NINTH COMMANDMENT. 111

(1) Maintain the truth of God, the glorious gospel, as he has revealed it (1 John 2 : 22 ; 5 : 10).

(2) To be regulated by truth in all our mutual transactions (Prov. 26 : 24, 25 ; Col. 3 : 9 ; 1 Cor. 13 : 6, 7).

(3) To preserve our own good name (Neh. 6 : 6–8 ; Rom. 3 : 8 ; 2 Cor. 11 : 1–4), avoiding hypocrisy (Luke 12 : 1 ; 1 Tim. 4 : 2) and false humility (Col. 2 : 18, 23).

(4) To defend the reputation of others by truth (3 John 12) and in love (1 Cor. 13 : 4, 5, 7).

(5) And to do so especially in witness-bearing: this may be (*a*) in private, repelling slander and testifying to good character (Ps. 82 : 3 ; 1 Sam. 22 : 14); (*b*) in public, as in Church or State courts, where judges, jurors, lawyers and witnesses are under oath to maintain truth. Under the third commandment we considered fidelity to the oath in relation to God, here in relation to man. Perjury is therefore a sin both against God and man (Deut. 19 : 16–19).

We are forbidden—

(1) To deny, distort, neglect or withhold God's truth (1 Tim. 1 : 19, 20 ; 4 : 1–3; 1 Cor. 16 : 22; Rev. 22 : 18, 19).

(2) To falsify. A falsehood is the utterance, in word or deed, of what is known to be untrue, with an intention to deceive and in violation of some right. These three things are important: If we state what we have reason to believe to be true, we may be mistaken, but cannot be false. If we utter an untruth with no intention to deceive, we may be jocose or ironical. If we intend to deceive those who have no right to expect information, as thieves or personal or national enemies, we are justifiable and skillful, and they expect us to conceal

our movements and to mislead them if possible (Josh. 8 : 4–8 ; Jud. 7 : 16–22). But when we intend to deceive those who have a right to expect truth from us, we break this commandment.

(3) To deceive by social lies, by exaggerations, half statements, mental reservations, "pious frauds," misrepresentations, etc. The object to be obtained, our convenience, amusement of others, the advance of the Church, or the good of the public or of the individual, is no justification (Rom. 3 : 8).

(4) To fail in fulfilling promises, even where it is to our own hurt (Ps. 15 : 4). A promise cannot bind us to do wrong to man or against God. If the promised action would defeat the result intended by both parties, the desired end should be secured in some other way.

(5) To be guilty of tale-bearing, detraction, slander, throwing suspicion on the innocent or clearing the wrong-doer, or anything prejudicial or injurious to our own or our neighbor's good name. (See Larger Catechism, Ques. 144, 145.)

5th. THE TENTH COMMANDMENT. OUR RIGHT TO CONTENTMENT. Ques. 79–81.

Q. 79. *Which is the tenth commandment?*

A. *The tenth commandment is,* THOU SHALT NOT COVET THY NEIGHBOR'S HOUSE, THOU SHALT NOT COVET THY NEIGHBOR'S WIFE, NOR HIS MAN-SERVANT, NOR HIS MAID-SERVANT, NOR HIS OX, NOR HIS ASS, NOR ANY THING THAT IS THY NEIGHBOR'S.

Q. 80. *What is required in the tenth commandment?*

A. *The tenth commandment requireth full contentment with our own condition, with a right and charitable frame of spirit toward our neighbor, and all that is his.*

THE TENTH COMMANDMENT. 113

Q. 81. *What is forbidden in the tenth commandment?*

A. *The tenth commandment forbiddeth all discontentment with our own estate, envying or grieving at the good of our neighbor, and all inordinate motions or affections to anything that is his.*

We have a right to contentment—that is, to the full enjoyment of our divinely appointed position, work and estate—without disturbance from our desires after the allotments of others, or from their feelings toward ours. It is our duty to preserve this right to others.

We should notice that while the other commands of this table of the law speak of acts, this refers to feelings or states of mind, and is therefore more spiritual in its form. The reasons are—(1) that as the last commandment it indicates that all require inward as well as outward obedience; and (2) that states of mind, which are unexpressed in conduct, have a moral character. This is a fit conclusion of the law, completing the circle of requirements, bringing us back to the spirituality of God, to whom we are accountable.

We should enjoy this right, because—

(1) Our position, work, possessions and changes are all determined by God (Mark 13 : 34; John 17 : 18; 1 Cor. 7 : 20, 22; Eph. 6 : 6).

(2) His object is declared to be his own glory and our good (Rom. 8 : 28; Eph. 1 : 12.) This includes our happiness, present efficiency and preparation for future service and glory.

(3) Afflictions and privations are parts of his wise and loving plan (John 21 : 19; 2 Cor. 4 : 17; 12 : 10; Phil. 1 : 12). They are chastisements to turn us from sin, or trials to develop our powers.

(4) Had we the talents and positions of others, we would be unfitted for our own work (1 Cor. 12 : 4–30; Eph. 4 : 11–13).

(5) God requires us to have child-like faith in him, and to be free from care (Matt. 6 : 25–34; Phil. 4 : 6; 1 Pet. 5 : 7).

(6) It is our privilege to co-operate with others for the good of all (1 Cor. 12 : 12–31).

We are therefore required—

(1) To have full contentment with our own condition (Heb. 13 : 5; 1 Tim. 6 : 6; Phil. 4 : 11). This does not check, but encourages, true ambition and the desire to increase our talents and influence, because—(*a*) Diligence in labor for such ends is commanded (Rom. 12 : 11; Heb. 6 : 10, 11; 2 Pet. 1 : 5). (*b*) Our condition is preparatory (1 Pet. 1 : 7; 5 : 10). (*c*) Opportunities are granted (Matt. 25 : 14–46). (*d*) Satisfaction with present attainments is always condemned (Phil. 3 : 12–14).

(2) To have a charitable frame of spirit toward our neighbors and all that is theirs—(*a*) As colaborers and helpers in God's service (1 Cor. 3 : 9; 12 : 14; 2 Cor. 1 : 24). (*b*) Delighting in their enrichment and efficiency (2 Cor. 9 : 8, 11). (*c*) Bearing their burdens (Rom. 12 : 15; 1 Cor. 12 : 26; Gal. 6 : 2).

We are forbidden to covet the persons, possessions or positions of others. This law does not prohibit a desire for that which is offered for sale, for places open to all, or for rewards promised to the diligent or to the most successful (Deut. 14 : 26; 1 Tim. 3 : 1; Matt. 20 : 26, 27; 1 Cor. 9 : 24). Nor does it hinder prayer for temporal or spiritual gifts, subject to God's will and the rights of others (Phil. 4 : 6). But it forbids all dis-

INABILITY. 115

content, haste to be rich, disregard of the rights of others, envy, jealousy, grieving at their exaltation or success, or lack of sympathy in their trials or of co-operation in their work.

Covetousness is an inordinate desire for that which has been given to others—a state of mind which is sinful, but does not of itself prompt to outward action. In this the tenth commandment differs from the other prohibitions, and has its own place in the Decalogue. Sin is a state of mind, as well as overt word or act. Covetousness may indeed lead to feelings elsewhere condemned, and to deeds of murder, lust, theft or lying.

The term "house" and the last clause, "anything that is thy neighbor's," mean the same—all his possessions. The specifications of persons and cattle emphasize the prohibition, and indicate the variety of the feelings condemned and the different claims violated.

The punishment denounced is fearful (Ps. 10 : 3; 1 Cor. 6 : 10; Eph. 5 : 5).

IV. ALL MEN ARE GUILTY AND HELPLESS. Ques. 82–84.

Q. 82. *Is any man able perfectly to keep the commandments of God?*

A. *No mere man, since the fall, is able, in this life, perfectly to keep the commandments of God; but doth daily break them, in thought, word, and deed.*

We have seen that the commandments are the expression of the divine character, and therefore cannot be changed. They require under all circumstances that man, created in the image of God, shall be perfectly conformed to his character in thought, word and deed.

We were taught, under Ques. 10, that "Adam and Eve, as created by God, were holy, disposed to and able to do right, yet mutable, and also able to do wrong;" and, under Ques. 37, that "the souls of believers are, at their death, made perfect in holiness," and are delivered for ever from temptation and sin. But since the fall and in this life, no one has been able to keep God's law. This is evident, because—

(1) All are "conceived in sin," and "go astray as soon as they be born" (Ps. 51 : 5; 58 : 3).

(2) "There is none righteous, no, not one" (Rom. 3 : 9, 10, 23; 5 : 12; Eccles. 7 : 20; 1 Kings 8 : 46).

(3) Regeneration by the Holy Ghost is declared to be necessary (John 1 : 12, 13; 3 : 3–8; 6 : 44; 1 Cor. 2 : 14; Tit. 3 : 5; Ps. 51 : 10).

(4) Even believers and the best saints, as Abraham, Moses, David, Paul and John, were defiled with sin (Gen. 12 : 13; Num. 20 : 12; Ps. 51; 1 Tim. 1 : 15; 1 John 1 : 8–10; James 3 : 2).

(5) Often when they would, they could not, do good (Rom. 7 : 14–24).

(6) We are all conscious of sin (Rom. 3 : 19; 7 : 24; 1 John 3 : 20), and have "secret" (unknown) sins (Ps. 19 : 12).

This inability is—

(1) Not from loss of faculties. The mind, affections and will, with all the powers of the body, are retained. The conscience still speaks of good and evil. Free agency, to do as we wish, is ours under all circumstances.

(2) Nor is it mere disinclination, which must have a cause. There must be something abnormal in a bird

which is never willing to fly, and in man if not one of the race is ever, of himself, inclined to glorify God (Gen. 8 : 21 ; James 1 : 14).

(3) But it is a moral corruption of our whole nature, which involves (a) spiritual blindness of mind, (b) hardness of the heart, (c) perversion of the will, (d) a deadening of the conscience. (See under Ques. 18.) We are therefore said to be carnal and unclean (Rom. 7 : 14; 8 : 5; Isa. 6 : 5). If we be corrupt, our thoughts and actions, so far as free, also must be corrupt. Free agency is ability to act according to one's nature. God is holy and free in his holiness; the devil is free in his wickedness; and man, being sinful, is free in sinful thoughts, words and deeds. By regeneration we receive a new spiritual nature (see under Ques. 31), which is contrary to our carnal nature (Gal. 5 : 17; Rom. 6 : 6), and in sanctification gradually overcomes it. Since we have this complex constitution, all our deeds have a double character. Our most holy actions are imperfect, mixed with sin. And our transgressions are not without reluctance, dissatisfaction and regret, which the Holy Ghost excites and develops into repentance. While we are in this life there are in us remains of corruption, and therefore imperfection and sin are in all of our thoughts, words and deeds (Job 15 : 14; James 3 : 2).

Jesus Christ was not a "mere man." He was a divine person, with two natures, divine and human, both perfect; and he was without sin, though made under the law and liable to temptation (Heb. 4 : 15; Luke 22 : 28). In his freedom he was able to keep the law perfectly, and in him the Father was well pleased (Luke 3 : 22; 2 Cor. 5 : 21).

It is not denied that unbelievers "love those that love them," and do many things in themselves worthy of admiration, but neither in design nor in fact do they fulfill the law nor obtain the approbation of God (Matt. 5 : 20, 46 ; Rom. 10 : 3 ; Acts 5 : 3).

Q. 83. *Are all transgressions of the law equally heinous?*

A. *Some sins in themselves, and by reason of several aggravations, are more heinous in the sight of God than others.*

This is always recognized in Scripture and elsewhere, as indicated in the degrees of punishment apportioned to the several sins, and to the same sin under different circumstances (Lev. 24 : 16, 21 ; Matt. 5 : 22 ; 12 : 31, 32 ; 1 John 5 : 16 ; Ezek. 8 : 13 ; Luke 12 : 47). The heinousness is not to be estimated by man's judgment, which often differs from the Lord's. Sabbath-breaking God classifies with blasphemy, murder and adultery as deserving death (Ex. 31 : 14 ; 35 : 2).

Sins are aggravated according to—

(1) Knowledge (James 4 : 17 ; Luke 12 : 47).

(2) Intention (Deut. 19 : 4–6 ; Acts 26 : 9).

(3) The persons offending (Rom. 2 : 21–24 ; Gal. 2 : 14).

(4) The parties offended (1 Sam. 2 : 25 ; Num. 12 : 8 ; Ps. 41 : 9).

(5) The nature of the offence (Col. 3 : 5 ; Rom. 1 : 32 ; Matt. 18 : 17 ; Num. 14 : 22).

(6) The circumstances of time and place (Matt. 10 : 21–24 ; Prov. 29 : 1 ; Jer. 7 : 9, 10 ; 1 Cor. 11 : 20–22. See Larger Catechism, Ques. 151).

The most aggravated sin is the deliberate rejection of

THE DESERT OF SIN. 119

the salvation purchased by Christ and urged upon us by the Holy Ghost (Matt. 12 : 31, 32 ; Mark 16 : 16 ; Heb. 10 : 29).

Q. 84. *What doth every sin deserve?*

A. *Every sin deserveth God's wrath and curse, both in this life and that which is to come.*

Some sins are more heinous than others, but every sin is sin. There are degrees of punishment in severity, not in character nor in duration. The desert of sin cannot be determined by criminals. But God, the lawgiver, declares that every sin deserves his wrath and curse, which are often expressed by the word "death." (See under Ques. 19.) The law does, and must, demand perfect obedience: sin is any want of conformity thereto. The Scriptures, while not attempting to demonstrate to our apprehension the demerit of each and every sin, refer constantly to—

(1) Sin as, in its nature, antagonistic to God (John 8 : 34 ; 2 Pet. 2 : 19).

(2) Each sin as the manifestation of an inward corruption, which can produce nothing but sin, and which unfits us for God's presence and favor (Matt. 7 : 16–20 ; 12 : 34 ; Eph. 5 : 5).

(3) Death as the natural result of sin and its righteous judgment (Rom. 6 : 21, 23).

(4) God as sovereign, holy and just, denouncing his abhorrence and wrath against every transgression (Hab. 1 : 13 ; Gal. 3 : 10 ; Matt. 25 : 41).

(5) The punishment as everlasting, the just equivalent of an offence against God and of self-perpetuating sin (Matt. 13 : 41, 42 ; 25 : 41, 46 ; Luke 13 : 27 : Rev. 20 : 9, 10, 14, 15).

As we all have sinned, and are under sentence of condemnation (James 3 : 2 ; John 3 : 18, 36), and as Jesus Christ, "the only Redeemer of God's elect," has accomplished salvation (see under Ques. 20–38), we are now prepared to consider—

V. THE MEANS AND CONDITIONS OF SALVATION. Ques. 85–107.

Q. 85. *What doth God require of us, that we may escape his wrath and curse, due to us for sin?*

A. *To escape the wrath and curse of God, due to us for sin, God requireth of us faith in Jesus Christ, repentance unto life, with the diligent use of all the outward means whereby Christ communicateth to us the benefits of redemption.*

The redemption, procured by Christ's obedience of the law and by his enduring the penalty for sin, is a complete salvation. As it is sufficient for all and is adapted to the needs of each, God graciously offers it to every creature as a free gift to be received without price or merit (Isa. 55 : 1 ; Matt. 11 : 28 ; John 6 : 37 ; Acts 17 : 30). He has appointed means for obtaining it— none other will avail, a condition on which it may be received—faith in the Lord Jesus Christ, which is always accompanied with repentance. These two are the inward means. Of themselves they do not merit, procure nor prepare us for salvation.

(1) They cannot satisfy the law.

(2) They do not entitle us to the gift of God, which is not of debt, but of grace.

(3) They are graciously produced in us by the Holy Ghost (Eph. 2 : 8 ; 2 Tim. 2 : 25).

FAITH. 121

Faith and repentance are to be obtained only by the diligent use of the ordinances—the word, sacraments and prayer—which are the outward means appointed. "Faith cometh by hearing, and hearing by the word of God" (Rom. 10 : 12–17). These inward and outward means are therefore said to be necessary for salvation (Acts 4 : 12; Gal. 3 : 21). We need not consider what God might have done. This is his plan of salvation. Christ communicateth to us the benefits of redemption on the condition of faith, which is given through the ordinances. The only apparent exception is the salvation of children dying in infancy and of persons in like condition, whom God has evidently included in his covenants, whom Jesus blessed, and of whom he said, "It is not the will of your Father in heaven that one of these little ones should perish" (Matt. 18 : 14; 19 : 13; Acts 2 : 39. See under Ques. 20).

[I.] **Internal Means, Faith and Repentance.**
Ques. 86, 87.

1st. FAITH.

Q. 86. *What is faith in Jesus Christ?*

A. *Faith in Jesus Christ is a saving grace, whereby we receive and rest upon him alone for salvation, as he is offered to us in the gospel.*

Faith is that persuasion of truth which is founded on testimony. Thus it differs from opinions and from knowledge, whether derived from intuition, consciousness, experience or demonstration. As faith rests on testimony, its reliability depends on the character of him who testifies. We ought to have more confidence in the teachings of the astronomer than in our own observations of the stars, and in the declarations of God than in all human assertions.

Religious faith rests on the testimony of God.

(1) In the supernatural revelation, the Scriptures, (2 Tim. 3 : 16), and

(2) In the witness of the Holy Ghost in illumination and sanctification (1 Cor. 2 : 5-12).

If we be certified that the communication is from God, and that we apprehend the mind of the Spirit, we can have no doubt as to its truth. We must therefore know what God says before we can believe his declarations.

Historical or speculative faith is a mere assent to the revelation of God concerning events or doctrines, as "that the worlds were framed by the word of God" (Heb. 11 : 3), that Jesus is Immanuel, "that there is one God" (James 2 : 19). This is often called a dead faith; thus "the devils also believe and tremble."

Saving faith accepts and rests upon the truth concerning salvation. It is faith in the Lord Jesus Christ. God testifies that he is God—the Lord (Heb. 1 : 8, 10); that "he shall save his people from their sins"—Jesus (Matt. 1 : 21); and that he is the anointed Mediator between God and man—the Christ (Acts 10 : 38), as he is offered to us in the gospel. It includes a knowledge of what is believed, and a trust in it.

The object of saving faith is—

(1) Jesus Christ; not merely a doctrine concerning him, but the Person. It apprehends, receives, trusts him. Faith *in* and *on* Christ expresses a union with him, and a dependence upon him as a person, with whom we are identified and from whom we derive life (Eph. 1 : 13;

Acts 10 : 43; 16 : 31; 26 : 18; John 1 : 12; Gal. 3 : 26; 2 Tim. 3 : 15).

(2) His work. He is declared to be the Creator, Preserver, Lawgiver, Judge, the Teacher with authority, the Worker of miracles, the Friend of the afflicted, the Example, and the Helper. These terms refer only to the subordinate portions of his work, and do not involve salvation. His special work is that of the Mediator —of the Saviour from the sinfulness and misery of sin— which he has accomplished by his obedience and sufferings. (See Ques. 20–26.) Faith must receive and rest on this atonement (John 3 : 16; 6 : 53).

(3) His promise—not to teach us, nor to help us to imitate his example, nor to assist us to redeem ourselves, but to apply to us all the benefits of his finished salvation (Matt. 11 : 28; John 3 : 15; 6 : 47).

The Author of saving faith is the Holy Ghost.

(1) Faith is the gift of God (Eph. 2 : 8).

(2) It is the first act of the soul regenerated—enlightened in mind, renewed in will, persuaded and enabled by the Holy Ghost to embrace Jesus Christ. (See under Ques. 31.)

The results of saving faith are—

(1) The acts and operations of the Holy Ghost in justification, adoption and sanctification. (See under Ques. 33–36.)

(2) Communion with Christ, love to God and man, and repentance.

These are the invariable and necessary results of faith. They are not always clearly discernible by our consciousness, but should be developed by constant exercise, to our growth in grace and in joy.

There are degrees of saving faith. These do not differ in character, and therefore not in final result. The weakest faith, that receives and rests on Christ as the Saviour, secures eternal life in him; but its weakness renders us timid, liable to temptation, inefficient in Christ's service and unhappy.

Assurance of faith is often defined as the certainty of that which is believed, and assurance of hope as the certainty of our personal salvation. The first term, however, generally includes both ideas. The assurance of our salvation is not of the essence of faith. We may, while exercising true faith, have doubts as to its character. Assurance is our privilege, to which we should attain. It is the necessary conclusion of conscious faith. We do receive and rest upon Christ alone as he is offered in the gospel; therefore we are saved by him. We are conscious of faith, and God's promise is sure.

2d. REPENTANCE.

Q. 87. *What is repentance unto life?*

A. *Repentance unto life is a saving grace, whereby a sinner, out of a true sense of his sin, and apprehension of the mercy of God in Christ, doth, with grief and hatred of his sin, turn from it unto God, with a full purpose of, and endeavor after, new obedience.*

Repentance means a change of mind, therefore of thought, feeling and purpose, but generally includes a sorrow for the past.

Legal repentance is the change produced by the law, and by fear of the penalty, or of the consequences, of sin. It has nothing to do with salvation. Thus Esau, Pharaoh and Judas repented. There is in it no distaste for sin, but merely a desire to escape its punishment, and

REPENTANCE. 125

it leads to attempted reformation, and then to despair and death (Ex. 10 : 16, 17 ; Heb. 12 : 17 ; Matt. 27 : 3–5).

Repentance unto life is a sorrow which is the effect of spiritual life, and leads to everlasting life. It is a turning from sin, while conversion is a turning to God. Conversion is the beginning of our Christian life. Repentance is the continuous resistance of sin until we be perfect in Christ Jesus. Sanctification is the Spirit's work within us, making us holy. Repentance is the effect of this work; we hate sin and turn from it to God. It is intimately related to faith. Logically, it is the result and act of faith. Practically, however, they are both present in the first effort of the regenerated soul. In faith we repent; in repentance we apprehend the mercy of God in Christ. By faith we are entitled to heaven ; by repentance we are prepared for it.

It is the gift of God.

(1) It is so called (Zech. 12 : 10 ; Acts 5 : 31 ; 11 : 18; 2 Tim. 2 : 25).

(2) It is the result of the Spirit's works of regeneration and sanctification (1 Cor. 6 : 11 ; Eph. 5 : 16–18).

It is produced—

(1) By a true sense of our personal sins as offences against God (Ps. 51 : 4), deserving his curse (Ezek. 18 : 30–32), involving pollution (Ezek. 16 : 61–63), and possessing a power over us (Rom. 7 : 14–24).

(2) By an apprehension of the mercy of God in Christ, which is the recognition of God's love, of his willingness and ability to save us from our sin (Rom. 3 : 26), and our personal acceptance of his grace (Acts 2 : 41). Conviction of sin and faith in Christ must conjoin to produce true repentance.

It consists—

(1) Of a grief and hatred of our sin—an abhorrence of sin more than a fear of its punishment. The latter, at first, may be influential, but as the work of the Spirit advances the distaste and hatred of sin become more prominent and abiding (Job 42 : 5, 6 ; Ezek. 36 : 31).

(2) Of a turning from sin unto God. We must forsake sin (2 Cor. 7 : 11; Ezek. 14 : 6 ; Rom. 6 : 1, 2). This includes—(a) Humiliation and Confession to God (1 John 1 : 9); (b) Acknowledgment of wrong, and restitution as far as possible to those personally injured (Matt. 5 : 23, 24). This does not expiate the sin. The crime of theft remains after the stolen property is returned. If the Church has been scandalized, confession, more or less public, and submission to discipline should be made (Matt. 18 : 15–18; 2 Cor. 2 : 5–8; 2 Sam. 12 : 14). And (c) Reformation (Eph. 4 : 24–32).

(3) Of a full purpose of, and endeavor after, new obedience. The Spirit works in us "to will and to do of his good pleasure" (Phil. 2 : 13). But we are hampered by indwelling sin, enticed by the world and tempted by the devil. We must resist unto blood, striving against sin (Heb 12 : 4), yield to the Spirit's influence (Eph. 4 : 30; 6 : 13–18), and depend on the grace and strength of Christ (Heb. 2 : 18 ; 4 : 15, 16; Rom. 7 : 24, 25). This obedience is called new (a) as to extent—not partial, but to the whole will of God (Ps. 119 : 128); (b) as to motive —not selfish, but love to Christ (John 14 : 15); (c) as to strength—not our own, but that of Christ (Gal. 2 : 20); and (d) as to aim—not to be saved, but being saved to express our love to Christ and to seek his glory in the salvation of others (1 Tim. 4 : 8–10).

THE ORDINANCES. 127

[II.] External Means: His Ordinances. Ques 88–107.

These are—THE WORD, THE SACRAMENTS AND PRAYER. They are used by God, to communicate to us the benefits of redemption. They are to be used by us, to obtain the inward means and conditions of salvation—faith and repentance.

Q. 88. *What are the outward and ordinary means whereby Christ communicateth to us the benefits of redemption ?*

A. *The outward and ordinary means whereby Christ communicateth to us the benefits of redemption, are, his ordinances, especially the word, sacraments, and prayer; all of which are made effectual to the elect for salvation.*

Signs, wonders, miracles, a light from heaven, an audible voice, dreams, visions and peculiar providences have also been used as outward means. But they were chiefly to attract attention and to confirm the message delivered. Thus Paul was surprised near Damascus, but he was required then to use the ordinary means (Acts 9 : 3–7). Marvels are not to be expected, nor are they now necessary. God's ordinances have been completed, made known and confirmed. Through them God reveals Christ, and we are commanded by them to seek and receive him.

Ordinances are appointments by authority for the accomplishment of certain ends. Religious ordinances are divine decrees, and are therefore obligatory upon all, and cannot be changed by man.

They differ from laws—(1) in that they do not depend on the nature of God, but upon his will; and (2) they are rules not for life, but for worship. They are therefore called "means of grace," the divinely-appointed methods for the bestowing and receiving of God's gifts. "It pleased God by the foolishness of preaching to save them that believe" (1 Cor. 1 : 21). The obligation is, however, the same: the neglect of them is sin (Lev. 18 : 4). They are God's method of communicating salvation, which can be obtained in no other way. "Faith cometh by hearing, and hearing by the word of God" (Rom. 10 : 17). Though necessary, they have in themselves no efficiency. They are means to an end. Their use does not necessarily accomplish the result. The efficiency is of the Spirit, who worketh through them in producing in us faith and repentance.

They are the word, sacraments and prayer, the means of communication between God and man. They are intimately connected, and must not be separated. All are required to be used. In the word God reveals his will for our salvation; in the sacraments he illustrates and seals it; in prayer we ask and receive it.

1st. THE WORD. Ques. 89, 90.

Q. 89. *How is the word made effectual to salvation?*

A. *The Spirit of God maketh the reading, but especially the preaching of the word, an effectual means of convincing and converting sinners, and of building them up in holiness and comfort through faith unto salvation.*

Q. 90. *How is the word to be read and heard, that it may become effectual to salvation?*

A. *That the word may become effectual unto salvation, we must attend thereunto with diligence, preparation, and prayer; receive it with faith and love, lay it up in our hearts, and practice it in our lives.*

Regeneration is the beginning and sanctification

THE WORD. 129

the continuance of the application of salvation to us. (See under Ques. 31–35.) They are the operations of God. He does not, however, "of stones raise up children to Abraham," but uses means adapted alike to his work and to our nature.

The word of God (See under Ques. 2.) (1) This makes known the charge of sin with its penalty, and Jesus Christ and his redemption, while the Spirit enlightens, " persuades and enables us to embrace Jesus Christ freely offered to us in the gospel" (John 5 : 39 ; Acts 16 : 14). (2) It reveals God's holiness, and our obligation to be perfect as he is perfect (Matt. 5 : 48), while the Spirit fills us " with grief and hatred of sin, and turns us from it to God, with full purpose of, and endeavor after, new obedience" (John 17 : 17, 19 ; 1 Pet. 1 : 22). This is God's method. He operates only through this channel. (In regard to infants see page 121.)

On the other hand, faith with repentance is the one and essential condition of salvation. But we are conscious that we cannot regenerate ourselves nor exercise these graces. They can be produced only by the knowledge and application of the truth. Here God and man meet. He restricts his operations to means which are within our ability. We can hear and read his word, "which is the power of God unto salvation" (Rom. 1 : 16).

The efficacy is not in the word, as it was not in the clay on the eyes of the blind man. (1) Sometimes it is unfruitful, or a stumbling-block, or a savor of death unto death (Matt. 13 : 19–22 ; 1 Cor. 1 : 18, 23 ; 2 Cor. 2 : 16). (2) It is often misused, as in temptation, by false teachers and through ignorance (Matt. 4 : 6 ; 2 Cor.

2 : 17 ; 2 Pet. 3 : 16). (3) It is the means. The Spirit is the agent (Eph. 6 : 17). (4) And the Spirit, as personal and sovereign, uses it (1 Cor. 1 : 24–31 ; 3 : 6). He should therefore be invoked to apply it to us (Ps. 119 : 18).

This means should be used—

(1) In personal study (John 5 : 39 ; Acts 17 : 11).

(2) In public preaching, by ministers called of God and authorized by the Church (Eph. 4 : 11, 12; 2 Tim. 2 : 2). The special efficacy of the word when preached is because (*a*) it is God's chosen ordinance (1 Cor. 1 : 21); (*b*) of the office, authority and blessing given to his ministers (Matt. 28 : 19, 20); (*c*) of the testimony, example, sympathy and prayers of those who preach (Gal. 1 : 15, 16 ; Col. 1 : 28; Eph. 1 : 16–23); (*d*) of the influence of the hearers on each other (Mal. 3 : 16; Heb. 3 : 12, 13).

The manner of its use is described fully in the Larger Catechism, Ques. 156–160. We may emphasize (1) the regular attendance upon all services of the church (Heb. 10 : 25), and the systematic, social and personal study of the word (Rev. 1 : 3 ; Isa. 34 : 16); (2) a preparation by prayer (Acts 1 : 14); (3) a personal application with faith and love (Acts 8 : 30; Ps. 119 : 97); and (4) a practical obedience of the truth (James 1 : 21, 22).

2d. THE SACRAMENTS. Ques. 91–97.

Q. 91. *How do the sacraments become effectual means of salvation?*

A. *The sacraments become effectual means of salvation, not from any virtue in them, or in him that doth administer them, but only by the blessing of Christ, and the working of his Spirit in them that by faith receive them.*

Q. 92. *What is a sacrament?*

THE SACRAMENTS.

A. *A sacrament is a holy ordinance instituted by Christ; wherein, by sensible signs, Christ and the benefits of the new covenant are represented, sealed, and applied to believers.*

The word "sacrament" is not used in the Scriptures, but was adopted by the Western churches as indicating the sacred obligation of these ordinances. The Eastern churches called them "mysteries," as showing that these external services have a hidden and spiritual meaning.

The above definition involves—

(1) Appointment by Christ (Matt. 28 : 19 ; 26 : 26, 27 ; 1 Cor. 11 : 23). The apostles added none, nor has the Church authority to do so.

(2) The use of sensible signs signifying spiritual graces. The elements are (*a*) water applied in the name of the Trinity, indicating the cleansing operation of God ; (*b*) bread broken and (*c*) wine poured out, expressing the suffering and death of Christ in our stead, and the removal of our curse.

(3) A real connection between the signs and the grace signified (John 6 : 56 ; Acts 22 : 16). God testifies that redemption has been accomplished and that he will apply it; and we accept and appropriate the benefits thus presented. This is evident in (*a*) the natural fitness of the signs, (*b*) the manner of their use, and (*c*) the appointment by Christ.

(4) Perpetual observance (Matt. 28 : 19, 20 ; 1 Cor. 11 : 26).

As means of grace the sacraments differ from the word.

(1) They teach only a part of divine truth—the results of Christ's work in cleansing and nourishing.

(2) They depend upon the word, without which they cannot be understood.

(3) They are designed chiefly for those who believe. For, while they symbolize the need, work, offer and application of redemption, only believers partake, and to them the benefits are represented, sealed and applied.

(4) Their necessity is not absolute in the same sense. We cannot believe without the truth, but the thief was saved without any sacrament (Luke 23 : 43). The apostles, Cornelius and others received the Holy Ghost before baptism (Acts 10 : 47). Their necessity arises from (a) the command of Christ; (b) their design as the method of confessing Christ, the marks of discipleship, the expression of Christian union, the means of developing our oneness with Christ, our growth in grace and comfort, and our communion with each other.

Their efficacy is their ability to communicate to us Christ and the benefits of redemption. This they accomplish by—

(1) Representing Christ. They speak only of him, the manner of his working—by a vicarious sacrifice of himself—and the effect on us in cleansing and saving.

(2) Sealing. A seal authenticates and confirms. (a) God acknowledges the salvation to be divine, and therefore perfect, and he pledges himself to bestow the blessings stated in the covenant. (b) We accept the covenant, become a party in it, engage to observe its terms, and claim its benefits (Rom. 6 : 3, 4 ; Gal. 3 : 27).

And (3) applying. The Confession of Faith and the Larger Catechism use the old English word "exhibit," from the Latin *exhibere*, meaning to administer

THE EFFICACY OF THE SACRAMENTS. 133

confer or apply. In partaking of the signs we by faith commune with Christ, and he confers his benefits.

This efficacy is—

(1) Not because of any virtue in them. Simon was "in the bond of iniquity," although baptized (Acts 8 : 20–23), and the Corinthians were "eating and drinking judgment to themselves" while at the Lord's Supper (1 Cor. 11 : 20–30).

(2) Nor in the elements. They remain water, bread and wine, and have no charm nor spiritual power. The consecration sets them apart from a common to a holy use as outward signs, but does not change their nature or character.

(3) Nor in the administrator. He should be an ordained minister (Matt. 28 : 19; 1 Cor. 4 : 1; 11 : 23; Heb. 5 : 4), but he has no miraculous gifts nor spiritual powers. He represents Christ, but cannot do his divine work.

But (4) because of the "blessing of Christ," who is present to commune with us and to impart his favors; and the working of the Spirit, who increases our faith and repentance, and takes of the things of Christ and shows them unto us (John 16 : 14; 1 Cor. 6 : 11).

The recipients of this efficacy must exercise faith, which is (1) a prerequisite to partaking of the sacraments (Acts 8 : 37; 1 Cor. 11 : 28); (2) that which looks beyond the sign, and apprehends Christ and his grace (1 Cor. 10 : 16, 17); and (3) that through which the Spirit alone operates.

The efficacy is therefore not tied to the moment of administration, but, depending on faith, is operative whenever, by anticipation, meditation or remembrance, faith is exercised (Acts 8 : 13, 24. See the first administration of the Lord's Supper).

Their validity refers to what is essential to their proper observance.

(1) The administrator must be an ordained minister (Matt. 28 : 19; 1 Cor. 4 : 1; 11 : 23; Heb. 5 : 4). This is orderly, and should be insisted upon, yet the validity depends more on the faith of the recipient. The sacraments, like the word, may be blessed to us even if the administrator acts presumptuously or in pretense (Phil. 1 : 15–18).

(2) The appointed elements must be used—water, bread and wine. Nothing can be substituted for these.

(3) These elements must be used according to Christ's direction. Water must be applied in the name of the Father, Son and Holy Ghost. The bread must be broken and the wine poured out, and both partaken of by all, and not merely by the minister.

(4) Those engaged must intend to profess and receive Christ and his divine salvation. If the services be observed in jest or in denial of their real meaning, they are not sacraments.

Q. 93. *Which are the sacraments of the New Testament?*

A. *The sacraments of the New Testament are baptism and the Lord's Supper.*

Of all the ordinances in the Christian Church, only baptism and the Lord's Supper have the characteristics above described. They closely correspond to the two sacraments of the Old Testament dispensation—Circumcision and the Passover. There has been but one plan of salvation, less or more clearly revealed. The seals of the one covenant of grace have at times differed in form, but not in substance, design or effect. (1) They have always been "the seals of the righteousness of the faith" (Rom. 4 : 11). (2) The outward services always signified and pledged a spiritual change (Deut. 10 : 16; 30 : 6; John 3 : 5; 1 Cor. 5 : 7, 8). (3) The condition for participation under both dispensations has been faith in the Messiah—Christ. The form of the seals differs. (1) They were typical and prophetic of blood to be shed; they are now commemorative, and show the effects of the sacrifice accomplished. (2) They were bloody, like the law which worketh death; they now exhibit the peace, purity and growth of eternal life. Baptism is the present form of Circumcision (Gal. 3 : 27, 29; Col. 2 : 11, 12), and the Lord's Supper of the Passover (Matt. 26 : 26–29; 1 Cor. 5 : 7. See also Confession of Faith, chap. vii. secs. v. and vi., and chap. xxvii. sec. v.).

A. BAPTISM. Ques. 94, 95.

Q. 94. *What is Baptism?*

A. *Baptism is a sacrament, wherein the washing with water, in the name of the Father, and of the Son, and of the Holy Ghost, doth signify and seal our ingrafting into Christ and partaking of the benefits of the covenant of grace, and our engagement to be the Lord's.*

Baptism is a sacrament, as above described.

The element appointed is water, which is used in the Scriptures as the emblem of (1) power, for good or evil (Ps. 42 : 7; Hab. 3 : 10, 15); (2) abundance and freeness (Ps. 65 : 9; Isa. 55 : 1; John 7 : 39); (3) life, present peace and eternal blessedness (Isa. 44 : 3; Ps. 23 : 2).

As partaken of, it indicates refreshment and new vigor (Isa. 55 : 1 ; Matt. 10 : 42 ; Rev. 21 : 6).

But as applied to the person, it always signifies purification—bodily, ceremonial and spiritual cleansing (Acts 22 : 16 ; Rev. 1 : 5).

Therefore the benefits here represented, sealed and applied to believers are regeneration and sanctification by the Holy Ghost (John 3 : 5; Tit. 3 : 5; Rom. 6 : 4). The recipients therefore profess their need of a spiritual change, their desire for that which Christ has secured, and their faith in his gracious promise. We have already seen (page 133) that the sacrament becomes effectual only through the power of the Spirit, and when we by faith apprehend Christ and his promise.

The mode of applying the water is not specified in the commission (Matt. 28 : 19), where the word "baptize" means the use of water for a holy purpose. Therefore, baptism is rightly administered either by sprinkling or pouring, or by immersion, provided the essential idea of purification is expressed thereby. The last (immersion) has the least to recommend it, and the first (sprinkling) is the scriptural method, as may be seen—

1st. In the use of the words "baptize," "baptism," etc.

(A) There are some passages which at first seem to imply another method, by the use of the words "into" and "out of." But (1) these prepositions usually indicate motion toward and from, and not interpenetration and emergence. At most they imply that the parties may have stood in the water during the service. (2) Both the baptizer and the baptized are said to have gone "down into" and come "up out of" the water (Acts

THE MODE OF BAPTISM. 137

8 : 38, 39). (3) The circumstances—the Jewish training of the people, the great multitudes baptized (Matt. 3 : 5, 6), the leaving the river Jordan for the springs at Ænon (John 3 : 23), the scriptures read to the eunuch (Isa. 52 : 15), the place a "desert" (Acts 8 : 26)—all demonstrate that the mode was by sprinkling.

(B) There are other passages in which it is certain that sprinkling or pouring was employed. This was the form of (1) all ceremonial washings (Num. 19 : 18; Heb. 9 : 10, 13, 19, 20); (2) baptism of hands, etc. (2 Kings 3 : 11; Mark 7 : 4); (3) that of furniture, tents and books (Mark 7 : 4; Heb. 9 : 19, 21); (4) that of persons "in the cloud and in the sea"—"dry shod" (1 Cor. 10 : 1, 2), in the ark (1 Pet. 3 : 20, 21); (5) all Christian baptisms: (a) three thousand in one night; (b) baths, tanks, pools are excluded, if they existed, because water once used in purification became unclean and therefore unfit for further use (Num. 19 : 21) : living or flowing water was required ; (c) they were performed in all places—in crowded cities, deserts, private houses, jails, etc. (Acts 4 : 4; 10 : 48; 16 : 33).

(C) There are passages which refer to the baptism of the Holy Ghost, which is always represented as descending, being poured out, lighting upon, coming as rain, snow, dew, cloud and fire; and from him we receive "the sprinkling of the blood of Jesus Christ" (Isa. 44 : 3 ; Acts 2 : 3 ; Heb. 10 : 22; Isa. 55 : 10 ; 1 Pet. 1 : 2).

2d. In the design of the service to exhibit the effects of Christ's redemption in purifying from sin.

(A) Among the Jews personal washings were by pouring water upon the hands and feet (2 Kings 3 : 11).

(B) All ceremonial purifications were by pouring or sprinkling (Heb. 9 : 13 ; Ex. 30 : 18, 19).

(C) Regeneration and sanctification are often so represented (Ezek. 36 : 25–27 ; 1 John 1 : 7).

Those passages which connect baptism with crucifixion, burial, resurrection, planting, engrafting, clothing, new birth, repentance, and remission do not indicate the mode of baptism, as is evident from the context and the number and variety of the illustrations.

3d. Sprinkling has always been recognized as valid by the Church.

The formula to be used is, "in the name of the Father and of the Son and of the Holy Ghost " (Matt. 28 : 19).

(1) This indicates our union with the several Persons of the Trinity. The Israelites at the Red Sea were baptized unto Moses (1 Cor. 10 : 2). John's baptism was not Christian. (*a*) He belonged to the Old Testament Church (Matt. 11 : 11–14); (*b*) the multitude became John's disciples (John 4 : 1); (*c*) the faith professed was in his doctrine of the speedy establishment of the kingdom of God (Matt. 3 : 2 ; John 1 : 26, 27); (*d*) his disciples becoming Christians were rebaptized (Acts 19 : 3–5). The Corinthians supposed they were baptized unto Paul, Apollos and Cephas (1 Cor. 1 : 12–16). In Christian baptism we receive God as our Father, Christ as our Saviour, and the Spirit as our Sanctifier.

(2) This involves "our ingrafting into Christ." Through our union with him we receive life (John 15 : 5 ; Rom. 11 : 17), and the Spirit which " communicateth to us all the benefits of the covenant of grace " (Acts 2 : 38, 39).

(3) It ratifies our union with those who are saved by Christ (1 Cor. 12 : 13–26). It is therefore often called

THE SUBJECTS OF BAPTISM. 139

the rite of initiation into the Christian Church. Those born within the covenant are hereby openly acknowledged as members, and those from the world professing faith in Christ are hereby welcomed.

(4) This union with Christ and his people involves "our engagement to be the Lord's:" (1) to live for him (Phil. 1 : 21) and to do his will (Rom. 6; John 17); and (2) to love his saints and to labor with and for them (1 Cor. 12 : 13, 21–27).

Q. 95. *To whom is baptism to be administered?*

A. *Baptism is not to be administered to any that are out of the visible Church, till they profess their faith in Christ, and obedience to him: but the infants of such as are members of the visible Church, are to be baptized.*

The subjects of baptism. This sacrament is the rite by which persons are recognized and welcomed into the visible Church. We have already seen (page 134) that the Church of God, founded on the promise of salvation by Christ, is the same under all dispensations. The Jewish Church was not a political but a religious organization. For a time the Church included the State. It was a theocracy. Its officers were God's representatives and the types of the Redeemer, and its subjects were the people of God. It was not more exclusive than the Christian Church, to which also belong the covenants, the law, the service of God, and the promises (Rom. 9 : 4, 8, 30). The door was open for the reception of all who would enter (Ex. 12 : 48, 49; Num. 10 : 29; Ruth 2 : 12), though no special effort to gather in the Gentiles was made until the salvation was accomplished (Matt. 28 : 19). The terms of admission have always been the same. Those admitted were—

(1) From without the Church. Under the Old Testament Dispensation these were comparatively few, but really they were of considerable number (Num. 15 : 14–16). They came from the Gentile world, and were called proselytes. They professed a personal faith in the true God and in his covenant to Israel, and promised to observe his laws and forms of worship. They were initiated by circumcision, baptism and a sacrifice. Under the gospel the same profession of faith and obedience is required (Acts 8 : 37). It must be credible; the candidate must show that (*a*) he understands the truth, and (*b*) is living according to it. It includes a profession of the fundamental doctrines of the Church as set forth in this service—(*a*) the Trinity, (*b*) the need of regeneration, (*c*) the efficacy of God's salvation, (*d*) adoption by the Father, (*e*) atonement by the blood of Christ and sanctification by the Spirit; and it is a consecration of self, time, talents and property to God's service. Of this profession baptism is the outward sign and seal, as circumcision had been.

(2) From within the Church. The visible Church has always consisted of believers and their children (Confession of Faith, chap. xxv. sec. ii.; Form of Gov., chap. ii. sec. ii.). Under the Old Testament the growth of the Church was chiefly from natural increase by births. Infants were born in the covenant, members of the Church, under its care, entitled to its privileges and subject to its government. Because (*a*) all God's covenants with men have included believers and their seed (Gen. 9 : 9–17; 12 : 2, 3; 17 : 7; Ex. 20 : 5; Deut. 29 : 10–14; Acts 2 : 38, 39); (*b*) the child and parent are by God considered as one. The political, social and

INFANT BAPTISM. 141

moral standing of parents determines that of their children. Circumcision did not make these infants Jews, but publicly recognized that they were born Jews and members of God's Church. That sacrament was the seal of the righteousness of faith (Rom. 4 : 11 ; Col. 2 : 11), and because of the faith of Abraham his household were circumcised with him (Gen. 17 : 9–14, 23–27). Thus also when a proselyte was admitted into the Church, all his were welcomed and received the same seal.

Under the gospel, the infants of believers should be baptized, because—

(a) The Church is one, in fact, covenant, design, membership, terms of admission, profession, obligations and privileges (Gal. 3 : 8, 29 ; Rom. 4 : 11 ; Heb. 11 ; Deut. 30 : 6 ; Col. 2 : 11, 12 ; Gal. 3 : 28, 29).

(b) Under the gospel there is an enlargement of its membership and privileges (Gen. 17 : 4 ; Isa. 49 : 13–23 ; 60 : 1–4 ; Rom. 4 : 9 ; 11 : 18–24 ; Eph. 2 : 11).

(c) There is no intimation that children are to be excluded. On the contrary, their membership is recognized by Christ in his treatment of them (Matt. 18 : 2–6, 10), in blessing them (Mark 10 : 16), in what he says of them and of his kingdom (Matt. 19 : 14 ; Luke 18 : 16), and in his charge concerning them (John 21 : 15) ; and by the apostles in declaring that they were included in the promise of the Holy Ghost (Acts 2 : 38, 39), in identifying them with their parents, in calling them "holy," as entitled to Christian instruction and privileges (Eph. 6 : 1–4 ; Col. 3 : 20 ; 1 Cor. 7 : 14), and in baptizing them.

(d) Households were received on the professed faith

of the head thereof (Acts 16 : 15, 33; 18 : 8; 1 Cor. 1 : 16).

(e) Infants need and can receive what baptism signifies --regeneration and sanctification (Matt. 18 : 10-14; 1 Sam. 1 : 28; 2 : 21, 26).

(f) Infant baptism was practiced by the early Christian Church, and has been by the vast majority of God's people in all ages.

There must be a profession of faith. Neither under the law nor the gospel was this made by sponsors or in the name of the children. The parents profess their own faith, promise to instruct and train their seed in it, and claim for them the blessings of the covenant. The faith of either or both of the parents brings the children within the Church, and makes them federally holy and entitled to baptism (1 Cor. 7 : 14).

By this sacrament infants are recognized as members of the Church, and as having a right to all its privileges, as soon as they possess the qualifications attached to each. They must profess a personal faith and have offspring, before they can present any in baptism. And they must have knowledge to discern the Lord's body before they can come to the Lord's Supper.

B. THE LORD'S SUPPER. Ques. 96, 97.

Q. 96. *What is the Lord's Supper?*

A. *The Lord's Supper is a sacrament, wherein, by giving and receiving bread and wine, according to Christ's appointment, his death is showed forth, and the worthy receivers are, not after a corporal and carnal manner, but by faith, made partakers of his body and blood, with all his benefits, to their spiritual nourishment and growth in grace.*

THE LORD'S SUPPER. 143

The Lord's Supper is a sacrament, as described under Ques. 92. It is called in Scripture—(1) the Lord's Supper (1 Cor. 11 : 20); (2) the Lord's Table (1 Cor. 10 : 21); (3) the communion (1 Cor. 10 : 16); (4) the breaking of bread (Acts 2 : 42); and (5) the cup of blessing (1 Cor. 10 : 16). These names express the character of the ordinance. So do the terms early adopted by the Church—(1) Eucharist, thanksgiving (see Matt. 26 : 27); (2) a mystery, possessing hidden meaning (see Col. 1 : 26); (3) the sacrament, the more significant and frequently observed (see 1 Cor. 11 : 26); (4) a sacrifice—the offering of Christ for us once for all, and of praise to him (see Heb. 13 : 15); (5) a love-feast, with Christ and each other (see 1 Cor. 5 : 8). The Roman Church calls it "the Mass."

It was closely connected with the Passover (see under Ques. 93)—(1) In its institution. "The same night in which he was betrayed" Jesus merged the one into the other, using some of the elements on the paschal table with the clearer gospel meaning (Matt. 26 : 26 ; 1 Cor. 11 : 23). (2) In its design—the commemoration of the deliverance from Egypt by the blood of the lamb, the remission of sin by the blood of Christ. (3) The one typical and prophetic, and the other memorial. (4) Christ is our Passover (1 Cor. 5 : 7).

The elements appointed are—

(1) Bread, which in Scripture signifies *nourishment*, that which sustains and develops life (Gen. 3 : 19 ; Matt. 6 : 11). Christ speaks of manna, the bread from heaven, to show its origin and the source of its power (John 6 : 50). He says that his body thus represented not only sustains, but imparts spiritual life and makes it everlasting

(John 6 : 32–58). The unleavened bread of the Passover was used in the institution of this sacrament, but no importance was attached to its being unleavened, and therefore the apostles and the Church generally have used the bread which is ordinarily eaten at meals.

(2) Wine, which is the symbol of *joy*. It was so used at social and family gatherings (Jud. 9 : 13 ; Job 1 : 13 ; John 2 : 3) and in thank-offerings (Ex. 29 : 40 ; Ps. 116 : 13). It is also used to indicate sorrow and suffering (Jer. 25 : 15 ; Isa. 51 : 17 ; Rev. 14 : 10) ; because it represents blood shed, either vicariously— Christ's death in our stead, or personally—our own sufferings, judicial, disciplinary or in Christ's service (Matt. 20 : 22). In the Lord's Supper it expresses thanksgiving for redemption. The wine used at the Passover and by Christ, the apostles, the early Church and by the vast majority of Christians in all ages was the fermented juice of the grape, the wine of the New Testament (Matt. 9 : 17 ; John 2 : 3–10 ; Rom. 14 : 21 ; Eph. 5 : 18 ; 1 Tim. 3 : 8 ; 5 : 23 ; Tit. 2 : 3). It has been a question whether it should be mixed with water as in the Passover. But we are not at liberty to substitute any other liquid for wine in this ordinance (Matt. 26 : 26–29).

As the elements signify nourishment and rejoicing— the effects of Christ's redemption, we profess to feed upon Christ and to praise him for our salvation.

The actions required are—

(1) The taking the elements, bread and wine, and blessing them. Jesus took and blessed or gave thanks (Matt. 26 : 26–28 ; 1 Cor. 11 : 23–29). This includes (*a*) The setting them apart from a common to a sacred

THE ACTIONS IN THE LORD'S SUPPER. 145

use as signs of the body and blood of Christ. This blessing does not change nor add to the nature of the elements, as that uttered at meals does not transform the food (Mark 8 : 6 ; 1 Tim. 4 : 4, 5). (*b*) Thanksgiving for what they signify—the accomplished salvation (1 Cor. 10 : 16, 17 ; Gal. 3 : 1). (*c*) The prayer that we may partake of the nourishment and joy indicated by them (Zech. 12 : 10).

(2) The breaking of the bread and pouring out the wine. The former is always distinctly stated, and the latter is implied (Matt. 26 : 26–28 ; 1 Cor. 11 : 23–29). These actions symbolize the manner in which remission of sins, spiritual life and nourishment have been procured—by the vicarious sacrifice of the Son of God. (See each record of the sacrament.) This is the divine, perfect and only plan of salvation.

(3) The giving and receiving the elements. " Take, eat," " Drink ye all of it." Both the bread and the wine are to be distributed to each and all of the communicants (John 6 : 51–56 ; Matt. 26 : 26, 27 ; 1 Cor. 11 : 28). This is the distinct command of Christ. Their reception, in the hand and mouth, signifies our voluntary acceptance of Christ's salvation by faith, the confession of our need of it, the profession of entire dependence upon Christ alone for pardon, spiritual life and growth, and our pledge to live by him and for him. As we all partake of the same bread and cup, we recognize our union with each other in the Lord, and promise mutual love, communion and co-operation in Christ's service (1 Cor. 10 : 16–22).

(4) The singing together (Matt. 26 : 30). This expresses the joy we have experienced in our union with

Christ and with each other in this service, in receiving the results of his redemption and in laboring in his cause.

The sacrament sets forth, therefore, not Christ's life, character, teaching or example, but his atoning death as the most important thing to be remembered and by which salvation has been accomplished. We are here the passive recipients of the free gift of God.

The efficacy of this sacrament has been considered under Ques. 91, and is indicated by the whole service. It is symbolical and memorial of the finished sacrifice of Christ, which by faith we remember, and in which by faith we are "made partakers of his body and blood, with all his benefits, to our spiritual nourishment and growth in grace."

Q. 97. *What is required to the worthy receiving of the Lord's Supper?*

A. *It is required of them that would worthily partake of the Lord's Supper, that they examine themselves of their knowledge to discern the Lord's body, of their faith to feed upon him, of their repentance, love, and new obedience; lest coming unworthily, they eat and drink judgment to themselves.*

The partaking of the Lord's Supper is a privilege and a duty, which belongs to those who are members of the Church, by birth or by profession of faith, and who have been recognized as such by baptism. But certain necessary qualifications are required of those who would enjoy this privilege and worthily partake of it.

1st. Those required by the Church. The power of the keys belongs to the Session, which is composed of the pastor and the ruling elders—the representatives of the people (Matt. 18 : 17, 18; John 20 : 22, 23; 2 Cor. 2 : 6–8). They have no power to decide who have been regenerated by the Holy Ghost. Their responsibility is limited to the judging whether the profession of faith be intelligent and credible—worthy of belief, and not denied by the outward life.

(A) In admitting applicants to the Lord's Supper the Session requires—

(1) Knowledge of the plan of salvation : (*a*) of their need of it as helpless sinners; (*b*) of the double nature of the Redeemer; (*c*) of the object and effect of his death; (*d*) of the offer of pardon as a free gift.

(2) Profession of a personal faith : (*a*) that they receive him as their Saviour; (*b*) that they rest upon him alone for salvation; (*c*) that they love and will obey him.

(3) Ability to discern the Lord's body, which includes—(*a*) the understanding the nature of the sacrament as appointed by Christ, symbolizing the benefits of redemption and the method by which Christ saves; (*b*) the recognizing by faith in the signs the body and blood of Christ; (*c*) the comprehending that the efficacy is due to the Holy Ghost.

All who have these qualifications should be admitted.

(B) At the administration of the sacrament the pastor should " warn the profane, the ignorant and scandalous, and those that secretly indulge themselves in any known sin, not to approach the holy table" (Directory for Worship, chap. viii. sect. iv.). Such offenders may be unknown to the Session and to all, except to God, but they are disqualified, and should be warned not to eat and drink judgment to themselves (1 Cor. 11 : 29).

(C) When any communicant lives inconsistently with his profession of faith, the Session should admonish and warn him, and if necessary should by regular discipline suspend him from the sacrament, until he give satisfactory evidence of repentance (Direct. for Worship, chap. x. sec. ii. ; Gal. 6 : 1 ; 1 Cor. 5 : 11 ; Matt. 18 : 17).

2d. There are other qualifications, of which each communicant must judge for himself. They concern his own spiritual condition and his relation to Christ. Before coming to the sacrament we should therefore examine ourselves—

(1) "Of our knowledge to discern the Lord's body" (1 Cor. 11 : 28, 29) ;

(2) "Of our faith to feed upon him" (John 6 : 50–58, 62–65) ;

(3) "Of our repentance" (Zech. 12 : 10 ; Acts 2 : 38, 46) ;

(4) "Of our love" (John 21 : 15–17) ;

(5) "Of our new obedience" (1 Cor. 5 : 8 ; 11 : 18, 19 ; Matt. 5 : 23, 24).

We should not be satisfied with the existence of these graces, but seek evidence of their growth, and we should come to the sacrament expecting by it to increase in them (Eph. 3 : 17–19 ; Phil. 3 : 11–16).

The word "worthily" does not mean with merit or holiness, but in a fit manner, according to the direction of Christ, with repentance for sin and faith in him for salvation.

3d. PRAYER. Ques. 98–107.

Q. 98. *What is prayer?*

A. *Prayer is an offering up of our desires unto God, for things agreeable to his will, in the name of Christ, with confession of our sins, and thankful acknowledgment of his mercies.*

Full and free communion with God was the sum of all the privileges of man in his original estate. It was forfeited by the fall. It was restored through the promise and accomplishment of salvation by Christ, to be enjoyed by us, in this life through the ordinances and by faith, and hereafter perfectly when we shall be with Christ and see him as he is. In the word he speaks to us, in the sacraments he manifests his presence, and in prayer we converse with him.

Prayer can be offered only to God. We are so directed in the First Commandment. (See pp. 88, 89.)

(1) There is but one God, and prayer is an act of worship.

(2) We can have spiritual access to none other, because of prohibition and in fact. Angels are sent to minister unto us (Ps. 91 : 11; Heb. 1 : 14), but with them we have no communication; departed saints are waiting to receive us (Luke 16 : 9; Rev. 6 : 9, 11), but they cannot return to us (2 Sam. 12 : 23; Luke 16 : 27–31); devils tempt us (Luke 22 : 31; 1 Pet. 5 : 8), but their presence cannot be perceived, and all pretended or attempted intercourse with them, or with spirits good or bad, is strictly forbidden (Lev. 19 : 31; 1 Cor. 10 : 20).

(3) Christ, who is God, is the only Intercessor, by virtue of office (Rom. 8 : 34; Heb. 7 : 24, 25; 1 Tim. 2 : 5) and as possessing merit or claim for the blessings desired (Heb. 7 : 25; Eph. 4 : 8).

(4) God alone has the control over nature, creatures, time and eternity, and the gifts of the Holy Ghost. He alone can preserve, defend, bless with temporal favors, and

bestow the benefits of redemption and the fullness which is in Christ (Col. 1 : 16 ; Matt. 10 : 29, 30 ; Eph. 3 : 14–19).

Prayer is personal communion. We, as individuals or as a body of persons, speak to this one God. And as there are three Persons in the Godhead, each of whom holds special relations to us, we pray to our Father in heaven (Matt. 6 : 9), we draw near to our High Priest (Heb. 10 : 21, 22), and we invoke the Spirit's guidance and comfort (2 Thess. 3 : 5). And these severally fulfill our desires. But, being one God, they must all be included in every act of worship. We can come to the Father only by the Son and through the Spirit (Eph. 2 : 18). The Spirit teaches us to pray, the Son indorses our petitions and claims his merit, and the Father grants our requests, which Christ bestows through the ministrations of the Spirit.

Our relation to God in prayer is—

(1) Not antagonistic. We do not come as enemies to defy, demand, negotiate or complain.

(2) Nor commercial, as strangers to obtain on some terms the supply of our needs from God's abundance, as Joseph's brethren went to him for corn (Gen. 42 : 10), or to condition services or offerings on the granting of our requests, as did Naaman and Simon (2 Kings 5 : 5, 15 ; Acts 8 : 18, 19).

(3) But submissive. We come in harmony with God. There can be no change in his character or will, but our rebellion and indifference are overcome. We recognize his authority, ability and love. We hold converse with him on his gracious terms. This submission includes—

(*a*) A "confession of our sins," as to their guilt, pollution and power over us (Ps. 32 : 5, 6 ; Luke 18 : 13), and a recognition of his readiness to forgive, cleanse and free us (1 John 1 : 9).

(b) A "thankful acknowledgment of his mercies"—that all his dealings have been mercies, favors to the ill-deserving (Phil. 4 : 6 ; Tit. 3 : 4–6).

(c) A recognition of his wisdom and of our ignorance as to our needs. We make known our requests, but expect him to do wiser and better than we can ask (Jer. 9 : 23, 24 ; 2 Cor. 12 : 8, 9).

(d) A claim for his love—that he will sympathize in all our experiences, and accomplish our real good (Luke 11 : 13 ; Rom. 8 : 28 ; Heb. 4 : 15).

(4) And familiar. Personally, we have no more claim than the prodigal (Luke 15 : 21), but because of the Father's love and our relation to Christ by faith, we are welcomed and may with all boldness ask what we will (Rom. 8 : 14–17 ; Gal. 4 : 7 ; John 14 : 13, 14).

"In the name of Christ" means (a) that we come at his invitation ; (b) because of our union with him we plead his merits and sufferings ; (c) being sons of God in him, we claim his love, privileges and inheritance as his joint-heirs (John 14 : 13, 14 ; 16 : 23, 24 ; Eph. 3 : 12).

The Spirit is called our Advocate, "who intercedes for us" (Rom. 8 : 26, 27), and we "pray in the Spirit" (Eph. 6 : 18). His work is within us, and consists of—

(1) Convincing us of our needs (Ps. 51 : 10, 11) ;

(2) Revealing God's attitude (Isa. 30 : 18 ; Ps. 65 : 2) ;

(3) Bringing us into harmony with God (Ps. 10 : 17 ; Zech. 12 : 10 ; Eph. 2 : 18) ;

(4) Creating within us proper desires (Rom. 8 : 26) ;

152 THE WESTMINSTER SYSTEM OF DOCTRINE.

(5) Guiding us in our utterance (Rom. 8 : 27).

Prayer should be offered (1) in private (Dan. 6 : 10 ; Matt. 6 : 6) ; (2) in the family (Job 1 : 5 ; Jer. 10 : 25) ; (3) with others (Matt. 18 : 19, 20 ; Acts 1 : 14) ; and (4) in the church (Isa. 56 : 7 ; Acts 2 : 42 ; 1 Cor. 14 : 14–16).

It should be—

(1) Personal (Gen. 32 : 11 ; Luke 18 : 13) ; and

(2) Intercessory (James 5 : 16 ; Eph. 6 : 18). This is a privilege arising from (*a*) God's love to us and others, (*b*) his method of carrying on his purpose of salvation, (*c*) our union with Christ, and (*d*) the relations which we sustain to others. The character of our intercessions is determined by our special relations to those for whom we pray. For the members of our families we plead God's covenant. For his ministers and the Church we urge his peculiar love and promise. For rulers we ask his guidance, as they are his ordinances and instruments. For our enemies we pray that he will change their hearts, as he has taught us to forgive them. And for all men we intercede because they need salvation and to them God has sent his gospel.

We may not pray for the dead, nor for those who are known to have committed the unpardonable sin (Matt. 12 : 31 ; 1 John 5 : 16).

All prayers should include adoration, thanksgiving, confession, petition, pleading and intercession. (See Directory for Worship, chap. v. sec. ii.) Yet the place, time and circumstances must determine which of these should be expressed or emphasized.

Prayer may be offered for all temporal and spiritual blessings. We are limited only by our knowledge and desires, and by God's will as manifested in his word and providence.

We should persevere in prayer, not with vain repetitions (Matt. 6 : 7), but with increasing importunity (Luke 18 : 1, 7; 1 Thess. 5 : 17). For prayer is designed not only to affect God, but also to affect us. God's delay in answering is often (1) to develop our faith under disappointments; (2) to increase our appreciation of the blessing, and our craving for it—as an undeserved favor; (3) to prepare us for its proper reception and use.

The efficacy of prayer, as of all the ordinances, depends upon Christ, and not upon the character or position of him who engages in it. Faith must be exercised, as in all the means of grace. Its weakness is our sin and shame, and may hamper us in our petitions; but its degrees and characteristics do not affect the efficacy of our prayer. Neither do united prayers increase the power. A special blessing is pronounced on these, because they unite God's children in sympathy, worship and work, and encourage faith, hope, love and new activity.

The answers to prayers are—

(1) Direct, without our personal co-operation. In the scriptural times God often answered by miraculous interpositions, but more frequently, as now, by directing the operations of the laws of nature (Ex. 16 : 13; Acts 27 : 24–44), by controlling the hearts and actions of men (Prov. 21 : 1; Dan. 4 : 35), and by the influences of the Spirit (John 14 : 26; 1 Cor. 12 : 4).

(2) Indirect, through our instrumentality. The blessings desired are often to be obtained only through the use of means. This is according to God's method in providence and to the terms of his covenant of grace.

154 THE WESTMINSTER SYSTEM OF DOCTRINE.

Bread comes through labor (Gen. 3 : 19 ; 2 Thess. 3 : 10), and conversion and sanctification through the teaching of the truth (Rom. 10 : 17; John 17 : 19). By prayer we invoke God's blessing on the use of these means.

Miracles were usually accomplished through prayer. They have been confined to three great epochs of history. The reasons for them do not now exist, and lying wonders are foretold (Matt. 24 : 24 ; 2 Thess. 2 : 9). The so-called "faith-cures," "healing by prayer and laying of hands" and "modern miracles" do not certify to the divine commission of the performer, nor prove nor illustrate his doctrine, and cannot therefore be classed with scriptural miracles.

Q. 99. *What rule hath God given for our direction in prayer?*

A. *The whole word of God is of use to direct us in prayer, but the special rule of direction is that form of prayer which Christ taught his disciples, commonly called,* THE LORD'S PRAYER.

Prayer is converse with God, and before we can commune with him we must know his nature and will, our relations to him and our characters and needs. But by sin we have been alienated from God, our minds are darkened and our consciences seared, so that we cannot form correct conceptions of him or even of ourselves. The word of God reveals all his perfections and our pollutions, his plan of salvation, his terms of communion, the spirit in which we may approach, the blessings we need and his bounty, the plea we may offer and the promises by which he encourages us. The whole word of God accomplishes this. The three great divisions of the Old Testament, the Law, the Psalms and the Prophets (Luke 24 : 44), correspond with the Gospel, the Epistles and the Revelation of the New. Each of these in its own way gives the information needed, narrates the experiences of Christians under various and peculiar circumstances, records numerous examples of acceptable prayer, and how God has answered (Gen. 18 : 23 –33 ; 24 : 12–19 ; Dan. 2 : 18, 19 ; Acts 12 : 5, 7–11 ; James 5 : 17, 18).

The special rule of direction is the prayer recorded in Matt. 6 : 9–13 and in Luke 11 : 2–4. It is commonly called the Lord's Prayer, because Christ taught it to his disciples. It was wonderfully suited to their use in the transition state between the Old and New Dispensations, containing no direct reference to Christ's atonement, not then accomplished. Yet, when interpreted by his death and resurrection, it expresses the highest thoughts and petitions which Christians can be prompted to utter. It is wonderfully simple and comprehensive ; a child can intelligently use it, and even the inspired Paul has no aspiration which is not included therein. Its petitions are really, but not formally, asked in the name and for the sake of Christ, because (1) the time for this definite plea had not yet come (John 16 : 24), and (2) it is only in Christ and with him that we can say "Our Father," and the words used are his own, in which he teaches us to pray for what he has procured for us.

It is a directory for worship rather than a form of prayer. This is evident in—

(1) The many variations in the prayer as given in the Sermon on the Mount and as repeated when the disciples said, "Lord, teach us to pray" (Matt. 6 : 10–13 ; Luke 11 : 1–4).

(2) There is no evidence that Christ, the apostles or the New Testament Church at any time used this prayer in public or private worship.

(3) No form of prayer is recorded in the Old or New Testament as enjoined, recommended or used by God's people. They always employed their own words as their circumstances and needs prompted.

Yet " it may be used as a prayer, so that it be done with understanding, faith, reverence, and other graces necessary to the right performance of the duty of prayer " (Larger Catechism, Ques. 187), and vain repetitions of it be avoided (Matt. 6 : 7).

Neither does it prescribe the order of the petitions, nor is it a framework in which our desires must be fitted. The prayers uttered by Christ and his disciples were not according to the order here given. They were most spontaneous and free in form and expression (John 11 : 41, 42; 17; Acts 1 : 24, 25 ; 4 : 24-30).

Its design is to show the "manner" of prayer, in what spirit, in what relation to God and his Church, and for what things we should pray. All the recorded prayers of Christ, his apostles and the early Church were in accordance with the directions here given.

Its unity is twofold :

(1) As to persons. On both occasions on which Christ gave this directory special reference was made to individual or secret prayer. Yet its very terms imply a conscious union with all the people of God in condition, need, desires, work and worship. We are also individually and collectively identified with God our Father. We are the subjects of Christ in his kingdom, and the

agents through whom his name is to be honored and his kingdom advanced by the Spirit.

(2) As to subject. The glory of God in the salvation of men. This is the one purpose of God in creation, providence and redemption. It includes all his gracious designs for man. For this he will be inquired of (Ezek. 36 : 37), and in its accomplishment he will use us as means. "Man's chief end is to glorify God and to enjoy him for ever;" and as colaborers with him in this work " we pray that he would enable us and others to glorify him" —that we, sharing in the work, may have part also in the glory. There can be no higher blessing, and it includes every possible temporal and spiritual good.

The natural divisions of the Lord's Prayer are those presented in Luther's Catechism, the Heidelberg and the Westminster—the preface, petitions and the conclusion.

1st. The preface: invocation, our relation to God and to each other.

2d. The petitions: the glory of God in salvation.

(1) As regards God.

(*a*) The honoring of the name—of the Father.

(*b*) The establishment of the kingdom—of Christ.

(*c*) The accomplishment of his will—by the Spirit.

(2) As regards us, who as colaborers need—

(*a*) Bread—temporal and spiritual nourishment.

(*b*) Forgiveness—from God and to others.

(*c*) Freedom—from temptation and the power of the devil.

3d. The conclusion: ascription of all glory to God, in which we are to be partakers.

THE LORD'S PRAYER. Ques. 100–107.

1st. THE PREFACE: Invocation, our relation to God and to each other.

Q. 100. *What doth the preface of the Lord's Prayer teach us?*

A. *The preface of the Lord's Prayer, which is,* "OUR FATHER WHICH ART IN HEAVEN," *teacheth us to draw near to God with all holy reverence and confidence, as children to a father, able and ready to help us; and that we should pray with and for others.*

Prayer is addressed to God, and must therefore be offered " with due apprehensions of his sovereign power, majesty and gracious condescension" (Larger Catechism, Ques. 189). This reverence is greatly increased and strangely modified by this new address or invocation. We recognize his immense superiority. He is in heaven, and we are on earth, with all that these terms indicate (Ps. 11 : 4; 123 : 1; Eccles. 5 : 2). Yet he is our Father, reconciled to us, loving us, delighting to commune with us, and more ready to give than we are to ask (Luke 11 : 13; Rom. 8 : 15).

He is "our Father," because—

(1) Of his own will he has made us sons (John 1 : 12, 13; James 1 : 18).

(2) Of our union with Christ. Out of Christ we were aliens and strangers (Eph. 2 : 12; Col. 1 : 21), but in him the sons of God (Gal. 3 : 26; 4 : 5; Eph. 1 : 5). Being one with him, we hold the same relation to his Father, and enjoy the same privileges—sons, heirs, coheirs with him (John 20 : 17; Rom. 8 : 17, 29; Heb. 2 : 11).

(3) This and all prayers are by, with and through him as our intercessor (Rom. 8 : 34; Heb. 7 : 25; 9 : 24).

"HALLOWED BE THY NAME." 159

(4) Being of his household, we are identified with his name, kingdom and will (Matt. 9 : 15; 25 : 34; Luke 22 : 28, 29).

(5) We are also united with all the children of God, and we must not only love them as such, and pray for them, but also, even in secret prayer, join with them in their desires and labors, saying, "Our Father which art in heaven."

2d. THE PETITIONS. Ques. 101–106.

Of these there are six. The first three have special reference to God, and the last three to us.

(1) AS REGARDS GOD. Ques. 101–103.

THE FIRST PETITION: THE HONORING OF THE NAME —OF THE FATHER.

Q. 101. *What do we pray for in the first petition?*

A. *In the first petition, which is,* "HALLOWED BE THY NAME," *we pray that God would enable us and others to glorify him in all that whereby he maketh himself known, and that he would dispose all things to his own glory.*

The "name" of God means his nature, character and relations as manifested in his ordinances, word, work and in the Person of Christ. "Hallowed" means either to render or set apart as holy—which in this case is impossible—or to make known the holiness which already exists. To manifest his own glory is the one purpose of God in all his works and revelations, and to glorify him is man's chief end.

This is to be accomplished by—

(1) The vindication of God. His name has been blasphemed (Ps. 74 : 18, 22; Isa. 52 : 5; Rom. 2 : 24), this part of his creation defiled with sin (Gen. 3 : 17; Rom. 8 : 20), his providence denied (Ps. 73 : 11; 2 Pet.

3 : 4), his plan of salvation ridiculed (1 Cor. 1 : 23), his Son rejected (Isa. 53 : 3 ; Matt. 21 : 39 ; Acts 3 : 13), and his Church persecuted (Ps. 2 : 2 ; Acts 8 : 1). He will vindicate himself, honor his Son and re-establish and magnify his authority (Ezek. 36 : 23 ; John 5 : 23 ; Eph. 1 : 20, 23).

(2) The manifestation of his glory—(a) in the plan of salvation (Rom. 16 : 25, 26); (b) in the Person of Christ (John 1 : 14 ; Heb. 1 : 3) ; and (c) in the characters and lives of his people (Matt. 5 : 16 ; 1 Cor. 14 : 25).

(3) His grace, enabling all men to appreciate his glory and render to him the honor and worship which are his due (Ps. 51 : 15 ; 123 : 1 ; Eph. 3 : 16–21).

THE SECOND PETITION : THE ESTABLISHMENT OF THE KINGDOM—OF CHRIST.

Q. 102. *What do we pray for in the second petition ?*

A. *In the second petition, which is,* "THY KINGDOM COME," *we pray that Satan's kingdom may be destroyed, and that the kingdom of grace may be advanced, ourselves and others brought into it, and kept in it, and that the kingdom of glory may be hastened.*

The kingdom here referred to is not his dominion as God over his works and creatures, but that described under Ques. 26, in contradistinction to the kingdom of Satan, who is called the god of this world, and whose power is to be destroyed by the advance of the kingdom of God (John 12 : 31 ; 2 Cor. 4 : 4).

The objects of this kingdom of Christ are—

(1) The destruction of the power of the devil (Rev. 12 : 9, 10) ;

(2) The deliverance of captives (Luke 4 : 18) ;

(3) The gathering a people to serve, glorify and

"THY KINGDOM COME." 161

enjoy Christ (Acts 15 : 14; Eph. 1 : 10; 1 Pet. 2 : 9);

(4) The making his Church glorious, including Jews and Gentiles, extending over the whole earth and perfect in holiness (Mal. 1 : 11; Rom. 10 : 12; Eph. 5 : 26, 27).

This is to be accomplished—

(1) Notwithstanding the great wrath of Satan (Rev. 12 : 12).

(2) In the face of the combined opposition, physical and intellectual, of nations and men (Ps. 2 : 1; Acts 4 : 24–30; 13 : 8).

(3) By spiritual influences (John 16 : 4–11; 2 Cor. 10 : 4).

The coming of this kingdom is not its commencement. The kingdom of grace began with the first promise (Gen. 3 : 15), was renewed in the family of Abraham (Gen. 12 : 1–3), was made a power among the nations under Moses (Ex. 3 : 6–10), and was developed as spiritual and universal as the "kingdom of heaven," by Christ (Matt. 4 : 16, 17; John 18 : 36, 37). We here pray for its coming with power unto every creature (Mark 9 : 1; Acts 1 : 8), and for its consummation as the kingdom of glory (Matt. 25 : 34; 26 : 64; Luke 22 : 16).

THE THIRD PETITION : THE ACCOMPLISHMENT OF HIS WILL—BY THE SPIRIT.

Q. 103. *What do we pray for in the third petition?*

A. *In the third petition, which is,* " THY WILL BE DONE ON EARTH AS IT IS IN HEAVEN," *we pray that God by his grace would make us able and willing to know, obey, and submit to his will in all things, as the angels do in heaven.*

The " will of God " here referred to is not his will in general, nor his decretive nor his providential will as made known in creation, in the moral law, or in his dealings with men, but is that which is concerned in the hallowing his name in the establishment of the kingdom of Christ, and which is accomplished by the Holy Ghost. In the second petition we pray for the external development and extension of the Church, and in this third for its internal growth.

The will of God is—

(1) Concerning his Church, that it should be (*a*) spiritual, not a mere external organization (Eph. 1 : 10, 22, 23); (*b*) pure in doctrine, forbidding false teachers, condemning heresies and declaring the whole counsel of God (Rev. 2 : and 3 :); (*c*) loyal to Christ (Acts 5 : 29–31 ; Eph. 4 : 15); (*d*) obedient to the truth (Gal. 5 : 7); (*e*) abounding in the gifts of the Spirit (Eph. 1 : 3; 3 : 16); (*f*) zealous in Christ's service (Tit. 2 : 14).

(2) Concerning each Christian, that he should be (*a*) conqueror of sin, temptation and remaining corruption (Matt. 5 : 48; Col. 1 : 12; 1 Pet. 1 : 15); (*b*) sanctified in all parts of his nature (1 Thess. 5 : 23); (*c*) furnished with the best gifts of the Spirit (2 Tim. 3: 17); (*d*) eager to manifest love by service (John 14 : 15 ; Acts 9 : 6), and joyful even to suffer for Christ's sake (Acts 5 : 41 ; 2 Cor. 12 : 10; Phil. 1 : 29).

Christ is the only standard after which we are fashioned by the Spirit. Yet the kind of conformity to the will of God to be wrought in the Church, and in us, is indicated in the obedience of the holy angels and of the saints in glory—with the whole heart, untiring and unending. "Thy will be done in earth as it is in heaven" (Ps. 103 : 20–23 ; Dan. 7 : 10).

These three petitions, therefore, are one—that God may

be glorified in the external and internal advance of Christ's kingdom. They are to be offered through all ages until every knee bows to the name of Jesus and every soul is perfect as he is perfect.

As we offer them in prayer we ask—

(1) That this great and glorious result may be accomplished;

(2) That we ourselves may honor God, be made and kept subjects of his kingdom and entirely conformed to his will;

(3) That we may be colaborers in this great work, the instruments by which it is to be perfected. Indeed, this is God's plan. It is the work which is committed to us by Christ. He saves by the saved. The Spirit convinces and sanctifies only as we teach the truth.

The responsibility and delight of this service remind us of our insufficiency, and we offer the remaining three petitions for ourselves. They are for blessings—not to enrich us, but to qualify and sustain us in seeking the glory of God in the salvation of men.

Our first need is strength.

THE FOURTH PETITION : TEMPORAL AND SPIRITUAL NOURISHMENT.

Q. 104. *What do we pray for in the fourth petition?*

A. *In the fourth petition, which is,* "GIVE US THIS DAY OUR DAILY BREAD," *we pray that of God's free gift we may receive a competent portion of the good things of this life, and enjoy his blessing with them.*

The plural "us" and "our" is used, because none is alone in this work. We have common needs, mutual responsibilities and sympathies.

By "bread" is meant—

(1) Not merely the necessaries of life, for it is never so used in Scripture.

(2) All temporal blessings. The only limitation is our apprehension of what is needed in this work and God's knowledge of what will promote our efficiency (James 4 : 15; 1 Tim. 4 : 4, 5).

(3) All spiritual favors. For here, as in the Lord's Supper, "bread" signifies the nourishment which Christ gives by the Spirit to sustain us in our several positions and duties in the Church (Rom. 15 : 13; Eph. 6 : 11, 12).

Our need is absolute and continuous. And we can appropriate only small portions, and at intervals, of God's bounty. "Give us this day our daily bread," or "Give us day by day our daily bread" (Luke 11 : 3).

It is the gift of God, undeserved and constant.

Without the strength which it affords we cannot continue in life, grow in grace, resist temptation or perform any service; but with it we can do all things (Ps. 19 : 13; John 15 : 5).

Our second need is pardon.

THE FIFTH PETITION : FORGIVENESS FROM GOD AND TO OTHERS.

Q. 105. *What do we pray for in the fifth petition?*

A. *In the fifth petition, which is,* "AND FORGIVE US OUR DEBTS AS WE FORGIVE OUR DEBTORS," *we pray that God, for Christ's sake, would freely pardon all our sins; which we are the rather encouraged to ask, because by his grace we are enabled from the heart to forgive others.*

This petition is closely connected with the preceding by the word "and," which implies either that forgiveness is as essential as strength, or that we need pardon day by day, as we do bread.

"FORGIVE US OUR DEBTS."

We have been taught, under Ques. 33, how God can forgive sins, and under Ques. 85 how we may obtain pardon—for Christ's sake and by faith.

We here plead for forgiveness, because—

(1) We are under the chastisement, pollution and power of sin (Ps. 130 : 3; Heb. 12 : 8; Rom. 6 : 16; 7 : 24).

(2) We are unworthy as sinners to be colaborers with God (Isa. 6 : 5; Matt. 3 : 11).

(3) We are disqualified by sin. We must be in the kingdom which we advance; we must testify of the grace of Christ (2 Cor. 5 : 20), and by our experience of its power influence others (1 Tim. 1 : 15).

We need to forgive one another, because—

(1) Such is the law and spirit of the kingdom (Matt. 5 : 44; 6 : 14; 18 : 21, 22).

(2) Being all united to Christ, there must be no variance among his members (1 Cor. 12 : 25, 27). We are constantly giving and receiving offence. But Christ has forgiven to each a far greater debt, and commands us to love one another (Matt. 18 : 27, 33–35).

(3) Colaborers must be in harmony (1 Cor. 1 : 12, 13).

"As we forgive our debtors" does not imply that our mutual forgiveness is the cause or the ground of God's pardon: it is the effect and evidence of his grace. Nor is it the measure of what we are to expect: our act is often partial and with hesitation, and even when full is imperfect; but God's pardon is always immediate and perfect. The two facts are intimately connected—as the one, so the other. If God has forgiven, we must. If we forgive, God has (1 John 1 : 9, 10; 3 : 14).

Our third need is deliverance.

THE SIXTH PETITION: FREEDOM FROM TEMPTATION AND THE POWER OF THE DEVIL.

Q. 106. *What do we pray for in the sixth petition?*

A. *In the sixth petition, which is,* "AND LEAD US NOT INTO TEMPTATION, BUT DELIVER US FROM EVIL," *we pray that God would either keep us from being tempted to sin, or support and deliver us when we are tempted.*

This petition is connected by "and" with the preceding. We sin constantly, because we are constantly tempted. That we may not continue to offend we pray to be delivered from temptation.

In Scripture "temptation" means—

(1) A test. Thus God tempts us, as Abraham (Gen. 22 : 1), to demonstrate our character and strength and to develop our graces. We, conscious of our weakness, shrink from these disciplinary trials, and pray that in them we may not fail (Ex. 33 : 15; Ps. 39 : 10–13; Luke 22 : 40).

(2) Enticement to sin. Thus we are tempted by the world, the flesh and the devil (Eph. 2 : 2; James 1 : 14; 1 Pet. 5 : 8); our communion with Christ is interrupted (1 Cor. 10 : 21); our attention to his loving commands is distracted (Luke 21 : 34); our efforts to advance his kingdom are opposed (Eph. 6 : 12); and we are induced to bring shame and damage to his cause, and even to aid the forces arrayed against it (2 Sam. 12 : 14; Rom. 16 : 17, 18). Conscious of our proneness to sin and of the fearful power of the adversary, "we pray that God would either keep us from being tempted to sin, or support and deliver us when we are tempted."

The petition implies, for our encouragement—

(1) That our temptations are under God's control. He

"THINE IS THE GLORY FOR EVER." 167

determines, according to our ability and the grace to be given, when, by whom and to what degree we are to be tempted (1 Cor. 10 : 13; 2 Cor. 12 : 9).

(2) He is with us in them. He as the Captain of our salvation "leads us into" and "delivers us from ;" and he intercedes for us (Heb. 2 : 10, 18; Luke 22 : 32).

(3) The result is certain. Satan shall be put under our feet (Rom. 16 : 20), his kingdom shall be destroyed (Rev. 20 : 2, 3, 9, 10), and his temptations only hasten on this glorious victory in us and in the world (1 Pet. 1 : 6, 7; Acts 4 : 26–30).

These three petitions include all that we need. We are confident that we shall be untrammeled and thoroughly furnished in our efforts to glorify God in the establishment of Christ's kingdom, because this is his purpose and work.

3d. THE CONCLUSION: ASCRIPTION OF ALL GLORY TO GOD.

Q. 107. *What doth the conclusion of the Lord's Prayer teach us?*

A. *The conclusion of the Lord's Prayer, which is,* "FOR THINE IS THE KINGDOM, AND THE POWER AND THE GLORY FOR EVER. AMEN," *teacheth us to take our encouragement in prayer from God only, and in our prayers to praise him; ascribing kingdom, power, and glory to him; and in testimony of our desire and assurance to be heard, we say,* AMEN.

This conclusion is omitted in the Revised Version of the New Testament, although it is found in many, and some ancient, authorities. It is certainly of great antiquity, and is very appropriate and scriptural. "Thine, O Lord, is the greatness, and the power, and the glory, and the victory, and the majesty" (1 Chron. 29 : 11; 1 Tim. 1 : 17; Rev. 5 : 13).

It may be regarded as—

(1) The summary of the prayer, the one desire expressed in its six petitions.

(2) The pleas urged for these requests. God is the only one who can fulfill them. The kingdom is his own (1 Chron. 29 : 11; John 18 : 36). All power is in his hands (Matt. 28 : 18), and the object to be accomplished is his glory (Rom. 9 : 23; 11 : 36).

(3) The ascription of unceasing praise from the children of the kingdom, as we sing on our prilgrimage and under every discouragement, as we labor and fight for the advance of the Church, and as we shall hail Christ when he comes in great power and glory, King of kings and Lord of lords, and when we shall reign with him for ever and ever. Amen and amen.

Thus concludes the Catechism. Having completed the whole circle of theology, it brings us back to the point from which we started, as we pray that in us may be accomplished man's chief end, which is "to glorify God and to enjoy him for ever."

"The grace of the Lord Jesus Christ, and the love of God, and the communion of the Holy Ghost be with us all. Amen."

QUESTIONS ON PART I.

I. INTRODUCTION.

1. WHAT knowledge was required by the early Church of candidates for baptism?
2. What catechisms were prepared at the time of the Reformation?
3. On what general plan were they arranged?
4. How does the Westminster Catechism compare with them?
5. What are its general divisions?
6. What does natural religion teach of God and man?
7. What is revealed religion?
8. In what sense is man a religious being?
9. What are the two great corner-stones of theology?
10. What is God's purpose in his works?
11. What is man's chief end?

II. THE WORD OF GOD.

1. What is the word of God?
2. What is the canon of Scripture?
3. How can the books of the Old Testament be proved to be genuine?
4. How can those of the New Testament?
5. What is revelation?
6. What is inspiration?
7. How far does it extend?
8. How did the ancient catechisms present the knowledge of God?
9. What is the creed called the Apostles'?
10. What is Hades?
11. In what order are the doctrines concerning God presented in the Westminster Catechism?

III. THE BEING OF GOD.

1. What is God?
2. What is the spirituality of God?
3. What are his attributes?
4. In what respect is God infinite, eternal and unchangeable?

QUESTIONS ON PART I.

5. Prove the unity of God.
6. What is meant by the Trinity?
7. What is a person?
8. Prove the deity of the Son.
9. Prove that the Holy Ghost is a distinct Person.
10. Prove that he is God.
11. What are the mutual relations of these Persons?
12. How do they co-operate in creation and redemption?
13. What is the peculiarity of the Nicene Creed?

IV. THE DECREES OF GOD.

1. What is meant by the plan of God?
2. What is its unity?
3. What are the decrees of God?
4. What is foreknowledge?
5. What is foreordination?
6. What is the sovereignty of God's plan?
7. What is its purpose?
8. How is it universal?
9. What is election?
10. How are men responsible for rejecting salvation?
11. Why should sinners be punished?

V. CREATION.

1. What is immediate creation?
2. What is mediate creation?
3. What were the days of creation?
4. How did God rest on the seventh day?
5. In how many states has man existed?
6. How did these differ?
7. How does evolution differ from the Bible doctrine?
8. How can it be proved that man was created holy?
9. In what did likeness to God consist?

VI. PROVIDENCE.

1. What does providence include?
2. In what three ways is it exercised?
3. What is the unity of providence?
4. What is preservation?
5. How is God's government carried on?
6. How is it related to his nature?

QUESTIONS ON PART I. 171

7. How is it consistent with the nature of creatures?
8. What is the object of providence?
9. What is a covenant?
10. What was the covenant of life?
11. Why was it called the covenant of works?
12. What was the test of obedience?
13. What was its seal?
14. What are the seals of the other covenants?

VII. THE FALL OF MAN.

1. What was the origin of sin?
2. How has the law of God been revealed?
3. What is the difference between holiness and sin?
4. What does sin involve?
5. How was man led into the first sin?
6. What was Adam's relation to his race?
7. Show that his headship was natural and federal.
8. What probation did angels have?
9. What is the advantage of federal headship?
10. How is this representative principle taught?
11. How does it secure salvation?

VIII. THE CONSEQUENCES OF SIN.

1. What is inherited depravity?
2. Prove that depravity is inherited.
3. In what does original sin consist?
4. What parts of our nature does it affect?
5. How does sin alienate from God?
6. What is death?
7. How does penalty differ from calamity?
8. How do these differ from chastisements?
9. Why must the penalty be inflicted?
10. How long does it last?

IX. THE PLAN OF REDEMPTION.

1. What was God's motive in the plan of redemption?
2. What relation had this plan to justice?
3. How was it of grace?
4. Who are the subjects of redemption?
5. What is said of the number of the elect?
6. How are all men included in redemption?

QUESTIONS ON PART I.

7. How does God deal with the elect?
8. For what are the non-elect punished?
9. What is the covenant of redemption?
10. What parts did the Father, Son and Holy Ghost take?
11. What is the covenant of grace?
12. What is a mediator?
13. What is a surety?
14. In what sense is faith the condition?

X. THE REDEEMER.

1. What is meant by the incarnation of Christ?
2. Of what did his human nature consist?
3. Is the personality of Christ in his divine or human nature?
4. What is meant by Person?
5. How long is this union of two natures to continue in him?
6. What relation to each other have these two natures in him?
7. What change took place at the death of Christ?
8. How is Christ present in heaven?
9. How is he present with us?
10. Why do the Scriptures speak of the "blood of God" and "the Lord of glory crucified"?

XI. MEDIATOR-PROPHET.

1. What is office?
2. How is the office of Mediator one?
3. How is it threefold?
4. Why must he be God?
5. Why must he be man?
6. What is a prophet?
7. How is Christ a Prophet mediately and immediately?
8. How does he work externally and internally?
9. What is illumination?
10. In what sense is Christ *the* Prophet?

XII. MEDIATOR-PRIEST.

1. What is a priest?
2. Prove that Christ was a Priest.
3. How did he differ from Aaron and his sons?
4. What was the meaning of the bloody sacrifices?
5. Why must the victim be perfect?
6. How was it regarded after the imposition of hands?

QUESTIONS ON PART I. 173

7. Why was it slain?
8. What victim did Christ offer?
9. How was the justice of God satisfied?
10. What is intercession?
11. What does Christ's intercession accomplish?

XIII. MEDIATOR-KING.

1. How does Christ's kingship differ from his authority as God?
2. Over whom is he King?
3. How does he exercise this office?
4. What is his Church?
5. How does he rule his people?
6. How does he exercise his authority over others?
7. How over material things?
8. What is his kingdom of power?
9. What is his kingdom of grace?
10. What is his kingdom of glory?

XIV. MEDIATOR'S HUMILIATION.

1. When did Christ's humiliation begin and end?
2. How was his birth humiliation?
3. How was his obligation to law?
4. In what respect was he made under the law?
5. How were his life, death and burial humiliation?
6. What penalty did he endure?
7. What were the incidents and culmination of it?
8. What do "Hades" and "Sheol" mean?
9. What is "Paradise"?
10. What is heaven?

XV. MEDIATOR'S EXALTATION.

1. When did Christ's exaltation begin?
2. How can his resurrection be proved?
3. Why is it important?
4. How did Christ ascend? and why?
5. What does his session in heaven denote?
6. What is he doing there?
7. When will he judge the world?
8. What is the general judgment?
9. Who and what shall be judged?
10. What books shall be opened?

11. What final sentences will Christ pronounce?
12. How shall the degrees of blessedness and misery be apportioned?

XVI. APPLICATION OF REDEMPTION.

1. By whom is redemption applied?
2. What is man's state by nature?
3. Why is this necessary?
4. What is the first act of the Spirit?
5. In this application what is the order of the soul's experiences?
6. Why is the Spirit called "the Lord and Giver of life"?
7. Why is he called "Advocate"?
8. From whom is the Spirit sent?
9. What operations are referred to him?
10. What is the completion of his work?

XVII. VOCATION.

1. What is the outward call?
2. Show that it is necessary for salvation.
3. In what does it consist?
4. Who are so called? and why?
5. What is the inward call?
6. Show that it is distinct from the outward.
7. Why is it necessary for salvation?
8. What is it called?
9. How are its subjects described?

XVIII. REGENERATION.

1. What moral influences of the Spirit are felt by all men?
2. What is effectual calling?
3. What does it accomplish?
4. What is regeneration?
5. What is conversion?
6. How far are we conscious of these?
7. By whom is regeneration effected?
8. What part of our nature is affected by it?
9. How are the results of this change continued?
10. How does regeneration differ from sanctification?

XIX. JUSTIFICATION.

1. What is justification?
2. Show that it is an "act," and not a work.

QUESTIONS ON PART I. 175

3. How is it a judicial act?
4. How are the claims of the law satisfied?
5. How does justification differ from pardon?
6. How does justification make us righteous?
7. What righteousness of Christ is made ours?
8. What is imputation of sin?
9. What is imputation of Christ's righteousness?
10. To whom is it imputed?
11. How does faith act in justification?
12. Show that justification is "free grace."

XX. ADOPTION.

1. What is adoption?
2. By what means are we united to Christ?
3. What is the difference between adoption and regeneration
4. How does adoption differ from justification?
5. How is justification distinguished from sanctification?
6. What is the influence of faith in adoption?
7. What is sonship?
8. What privileges belong to sons?
9. Upon what does sonship depend?
10. How long does it continue?

XXI. SANCTIFICATION.

1. What is sanctification?
2. In what two senses is "sanctify" used?
3. What are the inward means of sanctification?
4. What are the outward means?
5. Show that sanctification is a work.
6. How does the Spirit accomplish this work?
7. How do we co-operate with the Spirit?
8. What is meant by "common grace"?
9. What are the negative and positive fruits of sanctification?
10. What part of our nature is affected by this work?
11. When is perfect sanctification attained?
12. What is the standard of Christian holiness?

XXII. BENEFITS IN THIS LIFE.

1. What does faith involve?
2. What is the difference between faith and hope?
3. How does assurance of faith differ from that of hope?

QUESTIONS ON PART I.

4. Show that this assurance is our privilege.
5. What is "peace of conscience"?
6. Upon what does it depend?
7. What is "joy in the Holy Ghost"?
8. How is it promoted?
9. What is "increase of grace"?
10. How is it secured?
11. What is "perseverance of the saints"?
12. How is it secured?
13. How, then, do Christians fall into sin?
14. What are the effects of such falls?
15. Why are they not fatal?

XXIII. BENEFITS AT DEATH.

1. What is death?
2. How did death affect Christ?
3. What change takes place in the souls of believers at death?
4. How is it accomplished?
5. Where do our souls go at death?
6. Describe the intermediate state.
7. What and where is heaven?
8. In what does its happiness consist?
9. What becomes of the body?
10. What relation does it sustain after death to Christ and to us?

XXIV. BENEFITS AT THE RESURRECTION.

1. What is the resurrection?
2. What will be the order of events at the last day?
3. Who shall be raised?
4. With what bodies?
5. In what respect will they be changed?
6. What is a spiritual body?
7. Who will be the final Judge?
8. Who will be judged?
9. Concerning what will they be judged?
10. What will be the ground of acquittal?
11. How will the sentences be apportioned?
12. What will be the portion of believers?

QUESTIONS ON PART II.

I. THE LAW OF GOD.

1. WHAT is duty?
2. Upon what does it depend?
3. Why is duty unchangeable?
4. How has God made known his will?
5. Why is this will called the moral law?
6. Show that the word is the only rule to direct us.
7. How was the moral law revealed to Adam?
8. How was it taught by Moses?
9. How did it differ from the judicial and ceremonial codes?
10. What relation did it hold to them?
11. How did it differ from natural laws?

II. THE TEN COMMANDMENTS.

1. What is the sum of the moral law?
2. In what form was this given?
3. How is the moral law comprehended in the ten commandments?
4. What is the sum of the ten commandments?
5. What is the preface of the ten commandments?
6. How does God's nature require our obedience?
7. How do his relations to us?
8. How do his dealings?
9. Why is the singular used throughout the commandments?
10. By what rules should the Decalogue be interpreted?

III. THE FIRST COMMANDMENT.

1. How is the moral law divided?
2. How are the commandments divided?
3. What does the first table teach?
4. What is the first commandment?
5. How does it include the whole Decalogue?
6. What do the prohibitions include?
7. Why are we to worship God only?
8. How is God to be worshiped?

9. What is idolatry?
10. Why is communication with angels and spirits forbidden?
11. What is meant by "before me"?

IV. THE SECOND AND THIRD COMMANDMENTS.

1. What kind of worship must be rendered?
2. What form was given in the Old Testament?
3. How does that of the New Testament differ?
4. Is a return to ceremonial services lawful?
5. How is this commandment enforced?
6. What does "name" express?
7. What does "in vain" mean?
8. When are oaths lawful?
9. How do oaths and vows differ?
10. When are they not binding?
11. What is here forbidden?
12. How is the third commandment enforced?

V. THE FOURTH COMMANDMENT.

1. Why is one day in seven to be observed as a sabbath?
2. Prove it is still obligatory.
3. How is it to be sanctified?
4. What day is to be observed?
5. Prove that the first day is now the Sabbath.
6. By what authority was the change made?
7. What labor on the Sabbath is lawful?
8. What is the chief object of the Sabbath?
9. What other times for worship are required?
10. What reasons are annexed to this commandment?

VI. THE FIFTH COMMANDMENT.

1. How is the fifth commandment related to the two tables?
2. How may the second table be divided?
3. What is the design of human relationships?
4. In what sense are they divine?
5. Why is the filial relation specified?
6. What are personal relations?
7. What are social relations?
8. How are human laws to be obeyed?
9. How did Christ interpret this commandment?
10. What is its promise?

VII. THE SIXTH COMMANDMENT.

1. Why should we guard the life of the body?
2. How should it be preserved?
3. To what extent may we defend ourselves and others?
4. When is war justifiable?
5. What occupations are here forbidden?
6. What habits are forbidden?
7. How did Christ interpret this law?
8. Show that dueling, child-murder, suicide and lynch law are sins.
9. Why should capital punishment be inflicted?
10. What reference has this law to the soul?

VIII. THE SEVENTH COMMANDMENT.

1. Why should personal purity be guarded?
2. Show the peculiar heinousness of adultery.
3. How does Christ interpret this commandment?
4. How is the sin to be avoided?
5. How is celibacy to be regarded?
6. Under what circumstances is it commended?
7. What is the true idea of marriage?
8. How is polygamy presented in Scriptures?
9. What marriages are prohibited, and why?
10. When is divorce justifiable?

IX. THE EIGHTH COMMANDMENT.

1. Prove that the right to property is from God?
2. What is the province of civil law as to property?
3. How may property be acquired and used?
4. Under what systems has it been held?
5. How far has community of goods been recognized?
6. What is communism?
7. To what does it lead?
8. How is property now generally held?
9. How may it be used?
10. What are tithes?
11. How should we respect the property of others?

X. THE NINTH COMMANDMENT.

1. Show the importance of truth.
2. How does a liar stand toward God and man?
3. What is our duty as to God's truth?

4. What as to our own and others' reputation?
5. What is our duty in witness-bearing?
6. What is perjury?
7. What is falsehood?
8. When is deception justifiable?
9. When is it sinful?
10. When may a promise be broken?

XI. THE TENTH COMMANDMENT.

1. What is contentment?
2. How does this command differ from the preceding laws?
3. Why should we be contented?
4. Prove that this does not interfere with ambition.
5. What is covetousness?
6. Why is it sinful?
7. To what may it lead?
8. When is the desire for the possessions of others right?
9. Does this law affect prayer?
10. What does "house" mean?

XII. INABILITY.

1. Prove that we cannot keep the law of God.
2. What is inability?
3. What is it not?
4. What is free agency?
5. What effect has regeneration on free agency?
6. What on ability?
7. Why are Christians always imperfect?
8. How was Christ able to keep the law?
9. Can unbelievers do good works?

XIII. DESERT OF SIN.

1. What does the law demand?
2. What does every sin deserve?
3. Why must sin be punished?
4. Show that sins are not equally heinous.
5. How are they aggravated?
6. What is the most aggravated sin?
7. How are the degrees of punishment determined?
8. Are the degrees in the character or duration of punishment?
9. What is death?

XIV. THE MEANS OF SALVATION.

1. How was redemption procured?
2. Why is it offered to all?
3. By what means may it be obtained?
4. What efficacy have these means?
5. What relation have the outward to the inward means?
6. Prove that these means are necessary for salvation.
7. What is meant by the condition of salvation?
8. How are infants saved?

XV. FAITH.

1. What is faith?
2. How does it differ from knowledge?
3. What is religious faith?
4. What is speculative faith?
5. What is saving faith?
6. What is its object?
7. Prove that the Holy Ghost is its author.
8. What are its results?
9. How can they be discerned?
10. What are degrees of saving faith?
11. What is assurance of faith and of hope?

XVI. REPENTANCE.

1. What is repentance?
2. What is legal repentance?
3. What is repentance unto life?
4. How does it differ from conversion and sanctification?
5. How is it related to faith?
6. Prove that it is the gift of God.
7. How is it produced?
8. Of what does it consist?
9. How are we tempted?
10. How are temptations to be resisted?
11. Why is the obedience called new?

XVII. THE ORDINANCES.

1. What are the external means?
2. Show their relations to the internal.
3. What miraculous means have been used?
4. Show that these cannot be expected.

5. What are ordinances?
6. How do they differ from laws?
7. Why are they called "means of grace"?
8. What efficiency have they?
9. Show their necessity.
10. What relation have they to each other?

XVIII. THE WORD.

1. How do regeneration and sanctification depend upon the word?
2. What is the word of God?
3. What does it reveal?
4. How does it produce faith and repentance?
5. How may it be misused?
6. Wherein is its efficacy?
7. How should it be used?
8. Why is preaching specially efficacious?
9. How should we prepare for and apply the word?

XIX. THE SACRAMENTS.

1. What is a sacrament?
2. How do the sacraments differ from the word?
3. Why are they necessary?
4. What do they accomplish?
5. What is a seal?
6. Upon what does the efficacy of the sacraments depend?
7. Is it confined to the time of administration?
8. Why is faith necessary?
9. Upon what does the validity of the sacraments depend?
10. What sacraments had the Old and the New Testaments?
11. Wherein do they agree and differ?

XX. BAPTISM.

1. What is baptism?
2. Show that it is a sacrament.
3. Of what is water the emblem?
4. What does it signify when applied to the person?
5. What do the recipients profess?
6. How may it be applied?
7. What is meant by "into" and "out of"?
8. How were persons and things purified?
9. Prove that New-Testament baptism was by sprinkling?

QUESTIONS ON PART II.

10. What was the mode of John's baptism?
11. How is baptism by the Holy Ghost represented?
12. How does the design of baptism indicate the mode?
13. Show that "burial," etc. do not refer to the mode.
14. What is the formula of baptism?
15. What does it signify?

XXI. INFANT BAPTISM.

1. Show the unity of the Church.
2. How were proselytes received?
3. What are the terms of admission for those without the Church?
4. How does the Church grow from within?
5. Of whom does the visible Church consist?
6. Show that infants are members?
7. Why should they be baptized?
8. What household baptisms are recorded?
9. By whom are the vows and profession made?
10. Whose children may be baptized?
11. When may they partake of other church privileges?

XXII. THE LORD'S SUPPER.

1. What is the Lord's Supper?
2. By what names is it called?
3. How is it related to the Passover?
4. What are the elements?
5. What do they signify?
6. What actions are required?
7. What effect has consecration?
8. What does the reception of the elements signify?
9. What profession is thus made?
10. How is our relation to others expressed?
11. Upon what does the efficacy depend?

XXIII. PARTAKERS OF THE LORD'S SUPPER.

1. What qualifications are required by the Church?
2. What is a credible profession?
3. What knowledge and faith are required?
4. What is "ability to discern the Lord's body"?
5. Who should be warned from the table?
6. Who should be disciplined?
7. What self-examination should be made?

XXIV. PRAYER.

1. What is prayer?
2. Why must it be offered only to God?
3. What relations have angels and spirits to men?
4. Show that prayer is personal communion.
5. What is our relation to God in prayer?
6. What does submission include?
7. What is "freedom of access"?
8. What does "in the name of Christ" mean?
9. How does the Spirit intercede?
10. Where should prayer be offered?

XXV. KINDS OF PRAYER.

1. What is personal prayer?
2. Show that we may intercede for others.
3. For whom may we pray?
4. What pleas may we offer in their behalf?
5. For whom may we not pray?
6. What should all prayers include?
7. For what may we pray?
8. Explain God's delays in answering prayers.
9. Upon what does the efficacy of prayer depend?
10. Why is united prayer blest?
11. What are direct and indirect answers?
12. What are miraculous answers?
13. How is a true miracle to be recognized?

XXVI. DIRECTORY FOR PRAYER.

1. Show that we need direction in prayer.
2. How does the word direct us?
3. What special rule has been given?
4. Show the simplicity and comprehensiveness of the Lord's Prayer.
5. Prove that it is a directory rather than a form.
6. How may it be used as a prayer?
7. What was the character of the prayers in Scripture?
8. What is meant by "after this manner"?
9. Show our union with God and with men in prayer.
10. What is the subject of the Lord's Prayer?

8. What relation has the sacrament to growth in grace?
9. What does "worthily" mean?

QUESTIONS ON PART II.

11. What are its general divisions?
12. Into what two classes may the petitions be divided?

XXVII. THE LORD'S PRAYER.

1. What is the preface of the Lord's Prayer?
2. How is reverence here modified?
3. How does God become "our Father"?
4. What is our relation to others in prayer?
5. How is God's name to be hallowed?
6. What is meant by the vindication of God?
7. How does he manifest his glory?
8. What is the kingdom of Christ?
9. What are its objects?
10. How are these to be accomplished?
11. What is the will of God concerning his Church?
12. What concerning Christians?
13. What kind of conformity does the Spirit accomplish?

XXVIII. THE LORD'S PRAYER.

1. What do we ask in the first three petitions?
2. What is our responsibility as to the kingdom?
3. What are our three great needs?
4. What is meant by "bread"?
5. Why do we ask for "daily bread"?
6. Show that we need forgiveness.
7. Why must we forgive others?
8. Why do we constantly sin?
9. Why should we shrink from trials?
10. By whom are we enticed to sin?
11. Why should we pray not to be tempted?
12. What assurances have we of deliverance?

XXIX. THE LORD'S PRAYER.

1. Show the unity of the petitions.
2. What is the conclusion of the Lord's Prayer?
3. Why is it not in the Revised Version of the New Testament?
4. Show that it is scriptural.
5. How is it a summary of the prayer?
6. What pleas does it present?
7. How is it adoration and praise?
8. Show that this prayer is a fit conclusion of the Catechism.

INDEX.

ABILITY, 22, 116, 117.
Abraham, 39, 141, 161.
Adam—
 created, 22.
 descendants of, 22.
 fall of, 31.
 headship of, 27, 32.
 original condition of, 22, 24, 116.
 the Second, 45.
Adoption, 66.
Adultery, 104, 106.
Affliction, 113, 166.
Ambition, 114.
Angels, 77, 117, 149.
Anger, 101.
Assurance, 70, 71, 124.

BAPTISM, 134–142.
 benefits of, 136.
 candidates for, 5, 139, 140.
 and circumcision, 135.
 design of, 137.
 efficacy of, 136.
 element in, 135.
 formula of, 138.
 of Holy Ghost, 137.
 household, 141.
 infant, 140–142.
 mode of, 136–138.
 profession in, 140.
 a sacrament, 135.
 subjects of, 139.
Body, 103.
 after death, 75.
 at resurrection, 76, 77.
Book of life, 56.
Bread, 131, 143, 144, 157, 163, 164.

CALAMITY, 36.
Calling, 51, 59–61.
Canon of Scripture, 9.
Catechisms, 5, 6, 11.
Celibacy, 104, 105.
Ceremonies, 91.
Charity, 114.
Chastisements, 37, 113.
Christ—
 ability of, 117.
 ascension of, 55.
 death of, 49, 53.
 divinity of, 16, 45.
 exaltation of, 54–57.
 headship, 33, 40, 51, 52.
 human nature of, 42, 45, 54.
 humiliation of, 52.
 incarnation of, 42, 51.
 Intercessor, 49, 50, 55, 149.
 Judge, 56.
 King, 50.
 Lawgiver, 52.
 Mediator, 41.
 obedience of, 52, 53, 64.
 offices of, 45, 51.
 Person of, 43, 117.
 Priest, 47.
 Prophet, 46.
 Redeemer, 40.
 resurrection of, 54.
 righteousness of, 64, 65, 117.
 session of, 55.
 sufferings of, 53, 64.
 tempted, 117.
Christians—
 co-laborers, 163–165.
 free agency of, 117.
 imperfect, 73, 117, 163.

INDEX.

Christians—
  standard of, 162.
  strength of, 163, 164.
  tempted, 164, 166, 167.
Church, 44, 51, 99.
  admittance to, 139, 142.
  discipline, 126, 147, 148.
  members of, 140, 142, 162.
  officers of, 139.
  and State, 99, 107, 139.
  unity of, 9, 99, 134, 139, 141, 162.
  visible, 140, 161, 162.
Circumcision, 134, 141.
Commandments, 30, 82–115.
  interpretation of, 86.
  sum of, 84.
Communion, 143.
  with God, 50, 149.
Communism, 108.
Community of goods, 108.
Condition of salvation, 41, 120, 122.
Confession, 88, 126, 150.
Consecrate, 67, 144.
Contentment, 112–115.
Contingency, 19.
Conversion, 61, 62.
Covenant, 27, 29, 32, 37–41.
  condition of, 27, 28, 41, 120.
  parties in, 40, 140.
  of redemption, 39.
  seals of, 28, 29.
Covetousness, 112–115.
Creation, 17–21.
  object in, 8.
  days of, 21.
  of man, 22–24.
  new, 23, 59, 61, 66, 116, 128.
Creeds, 11, 12, 18, 59.

DEATH, 36, 74, 101, 119.
Deception, 111, 112.
Decrees, 18, 39.
Defence, 101.
Depravity, 33–35.
Desertion, 106.
Devils, 77, 117, 149, 167.
Discipline, 126, 147, 148.
Divorce, 106.
Dueling, 102.
Duty, 81, 82.

Duty to God, 86–97.
  to man, 97–115.

EFFECTUAL CALLING, 51, 61.
Efficacy—
  of baptism, 133, 134, 136.
  of Lord's Supper, 133, 134, 146.
  of prayer, 153.
  of the word, 129.
Election, 39, 40.
Evolution, 23.
Expiation, 24, 48.

FAITH, 41, 66, 121, 125.
  assurance of, 70, 71, 124.
  author of, 123.
  a condition, 41, 120, 129.
  -cures, 154.
  degrees of, 124.
  a gift, 20, 39, 123.
  a means, 67, 120, 125.
  object of, 122.
  and prayer, 153.
  religious, 122.
  results of, 123.
  and sacraments, 133, 134, 140, 142, 147, 148.
  salvation by, 20, 121, 122.
  saving, 122.
  speculative, 122.
Fall, 24, 31.
Falsehood, 93, 111.
Family, 99.
  prayer, 95, 152.
Foreknowledge, 19.
Foreordination, 19.
Forgiveness, 164, 165.
Forms of prayer, 155, 156.
Free agency, 19, 117.

GAMBLING, 109.
God, 13.
  attributes of, 13–15.
  being of, 13.
  communion with, 149.
  decrees of, 18, 39.
  definition of, 13.
  eternal, 13.
  Father, 158.
  foreknowledge of, 19.
  free agency of, 117.

God, glory of, 7, 8, 20, 159, 160, 168.
government of, 26.
holiness of, 14, 159.
infinite, 13.
justice of, 14, 49.
name of, 159.
purpose of, 7, 8, 19, 20, 159, 162, 168.
sovereignty of, 19, 20, 38, 50, 158.
spirituality of, 13.
Trinity in, 15, 16.
unchangeable, 13.
unity of, 15, 16.
vindication of, 159.
will of, 30, 82, 161, 162.

GRACE, 20, 38.
common, 61, 68.
covenant of, 41.
dying, 73.
efficacious, 59–63.
increase in, 72, 126, 129, 148.
in justification, 65.
means of, 128.

HABITS, 102.
Hades, 12, 53.
Hatred, 102.
Headship, 27, 32, 33, 40, 52.
Heaven, 54, 75, 107.
Holiness, 14, 31, 69, 159.
Holy Spirit—
 Advocate, 58, 151.
 baptism of, 137, 142.
 blasphemy against, 17, 119, 152.
 call by, 60, 61.
 divinity of, 17.
 and faith, 39, 123.
 grieved, 71, 73.
 joy in, 72.
 personality of, 17.
 quickens, 58.
 sanctifies, 68, 129.
 witness of, 71, 122.
 work, 57, 58.
Household baptism, 141.
Humanity of Christ, 43, 45, 54.
Humiliation, 126.
 of Christ, 52.

IMMERSION, 136–138.
Imputation, 64, 65.
Inability, 57, 116.
Incarnation, 42, 51.
Infant baptism, 140–142.
 salvation, 121, 142.
Inspiration, 9–11.
Intercession—
 by Christ, 49, 50, 55, 149.
 by Christians, 152.
 by Holy Ghost, 58, 89, 151.
 by saints, 89, 149.
Intermediate state, 53, 74.
Irreverence, 93.

JOY IN HOLY GHOST, 72.
Judge, 56, 63, 77.
Judgment, 51, 56, 77.
Justice, 14, 49.
Justification, 62–66, 78.

KINGDOM of Christ, 50, 51, 160, 161, 168.
 of Satan, 160, 161, 167.

LAW of God, 30, 81, 82, 99, 127.
 ceremonial, 30, 85.
 interpretation of, 86.
 judicial, 83.
 moral, 30, 69, 83.
 natural, 83.
 sum of, 84, 97.
 written, 30, 83, 84.
Laws—
 of health, 101.
 lynch, 102.
 of men, 99, 100, 107.
Life, 100, 101.
Lord's Prayer, 154–168.
Lord's Supper, 134, 142–148.
Love, 84, 88, 97, 103.
Lying, 93, 110.

MAN—
 chief end, 7, 159, 168.
 creation of, 22.
 descendants of, 23.
 fall of, 24.
 four states of, 23.
 free agency of, 19, 117.
 nature of, 7, 8, 22, 23, 57, 154.

INDEX.

Man, probation of, 23.
  will of, 23.
Marriage, 104, 105.
Means of grace, 120, 121–131.
Mediator, 41, 45, 51, 52, 123.
Miracles, 127, 154.
Murder, 102.

NEW BIRTH, 23, 58, 61, 128.
Nicene Creed, 18, 59.

OATH, 92, 93.
Obedience, 53, 84, 126.
Obligation, 81, 85.
Offenders, 147, 148.
Office, 44.
Ordinances, 91, 127–168.
Original sin, 32–35.

PARADISE, 54.
Pardon, 63, 164, 165.
Passover, 134.
Peace, 71.
Penalty, 36, 39, 119.
Perfectionism, 69.
Perjury, 92, 93, 111.
Perseverance, 41, 73, 167.
Person, 17.
Personality of Christ, 43.
Polygamy, 105.
Prayer, 68, 95, 114, 149–168.
  answers to, 153, 154.
  design of, 153.
  directory in, 154, 156.
  efficacy of, 153.
  and faith, 153.
  family, 95, 152.
  forms of, 155, 156.
  intercessory, 149, 152.
  Lord's, 154–168.
  and miracles, 154.
  in name of Christ, 151, 155.
  parts of, 152.
  perseverance in, 153.
  personal, 95, 152, 156.
  relation in, 150.
  to Trinity, 149, 150.
  united, 95, 154.
Predetermination, 19.
Preservation, 25.
Priest, 47.

Probation, 23, 27, 31, 33, 101.
Profanity, 92.
Profession, 88, 132, 134, 140, 147.
Prophet, 46.
Propitiation, 48, 49.
Proselytes, 140.
Providence, 8, 25–27, 51, 68, 166.
Punishment, 21, 33, 36, 56, 119.
  capital, 102.
Purification, 136, 138.

QUALIFICATIONS—
  for baptism, 133, 140.
  for Lord's Supper, 133, 146–148.

REDEMPTION, 8, 19, 23, 37, 38.
  benefits of, 62–78.
Regeneration, 23, 24, 59, 61, 62, 66, 116, 128.
  and baptism, 138.
Relation to God, 97, 158.
  to man, 97, 99, 100–115, 159.
Religion, 7, 8.
Religious experiences, 155.
Repentance, 121, 124–126.
Reputation, 111.
Responsibility, 20.
Restitution, 126.
Resurrection of Christ, 54, 96.
  of men, 75, 76.
Revelation, 10, 11, 82.
Reverence, 153.
Righteousness, 63.

SABBATH, 93–97, 118.
Sacraments, 68, 128, 130–148.
  efficacy of, 132, 133–146.
  elements in, 131, 133, 134, 143.
  qualifications for, 133, 140.
  validity of, 134.
Sacrifice, 48, 53, 145.
Salvation, 20, 38, 82.
  condition of, 41, 120, 129, 135.
  of infants, 121, 142.
  means of, 120.
  unity of plan, 135.
Sanctification, 59, 62, 66, 67, 125, 128.
  and baptism, 138.
  fruits of, 68.
  means of, 67, 123, 125–127, 148.

INDEX.

Sanctification, perfect, 69.
Satan, 32, 73, 167.
   kingdom of, 160, 161, 167.
Scriptures, 9, 68.
Self-defence, 101.
Self-examination, 148.
Services, 91.
Session, 146–148.
Session of Christ, 55.
Seventh day, 22, 94.
Sheol, 53.
Sin, 20, 23, 31, 32, 119.
   aggravation of, 118.
   estate of, 34.
   first, 31, 32.
   heinous, 118.
   origin of, 29.
   original, 32, 34, 35, 116.
   punishment of, 21, 33, 36, 119.
   unpardonable, 118, 152.
Slander, 112.
Socialism, 108.
Sonship, 66, 158.
Souls, 22, 43, 54.
   after death, 53, 54, 74.
Sovereignty, 19, 20, 38, 50.
Spirits, 87, 149.
State, 99, 107.
Substitution, 48, 49, 145.
Suicide, 102.

TEMPTATION, 32, 73, 126, 149, 166.
Testaments, 9, 134, 140.
Thanksgiving, 143, 145, 151, 167.
Theology, 12.

Tithes, 107.
Tree of knowledge, 28.
   of life, 29.
Trials, 166.
Trinity, 15, 16, 17, 39, 150.
Truth, 68, 110.

UNITY of the Church, 9, 99, 134, 139, 141.
   of God, 15, 16.

VALIDITY OF SACRAMENTS, 134, 138.
Vicarious sacrifice, 48, 49, 53, 145.
Victim, 48, 49.
Vindication of God, 159.
Vows, 93.

WAR, 101.
Water, 131, 135, 136, 144.
Will of God, 30, 82, 161, 162.
   of man, 23, 30.
Witness, 92, 110.
Word of God, 9, 10, 68, 128, 154.
   call by, 59.
   efficacy of, 129, 130.
   preached, 130.
   and sacraments, 131, 132.
   studied, 130.
Works, good, 118.
Worship, 97.
   form of, 90, 91, 155, 156.
   times for, 95, 152, 168.
Wrath of God, 53, 119.

THE END.

www.ingramcontent.com/pod-product-compliance
Lightning Source LLC
Chambersburg PA
CBHW051928160426
43198CB00012B/2080